Scott Foresman Reading Practice Book

Scott Foresman

Editorial Offices: Glenview, Illinois • New York, New York
Sales Offices: Reading, Massachusetts • Duluth, Georgia • Glenview, Illinois
Carrollton, Texas • Menlo Park, California

Credits

Editorial Offices
Glenview, Illinois • New York, New York

Sales Offices
Reading, Massachusetts • Duluth, Georgia • Glenview, Illinois
Carrollton, Texas • Menlo Park, California

ISBN 0-673-59695-8

4 5 6 7 8 9 10-CRK-06 05 04 03 02 01 00

Table of Contents

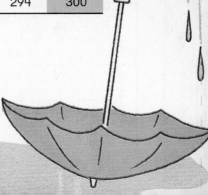

Family Times

Sing the Alphabet with Me

Aa is for an apple tree.
Bb is for a buzzing bee.
Cc is for a cat and can.
Dd is for my dog named Dan.
Name the letters that you see.
Sing the alphabet with me.

Ee is for an egg to eat.
Ff is for my face and feet.
Gg is for a goose that's gray.
Hh is for a horse and hay.
Name the letters that you see.
Sing the alphabet with me.

Ii is for an inch or two.
Jj is for a jet that's blue.
Kk is for a key and kite.
Ll is for a lamp and light.
Name the letters that you see.
Sing the alphabet with me.

Mm is for a mask that's mine.
Nn is for the number nine.
Oo is for an ox and otter.
Pp is for a pot and potter.
Name the letters that you see.
Sing the alphabet with me.

Qq is for a quarterback.
Rr is for a railroad track.
Ss is for the sun and sea.
Tt is for some toast and tea.
Name the letters that you see.
Sing the alphabet with me.

Uu is for that umbrella too.
Vv is for a vest that's new.
Ww is for a wig.
Xx is for an X-rayed pig!
Name the letters that you see.
Sing the alphabet with me.

Yy is for a yam for you.
Zz is for a zebra zoo!
We can sing our ABCs.
We can sing from A to Z.
Name the letters that you see.
Sing the alphabet with me.

Your child will be learning about the alphabet and identifying rhyming words. Say or sing the alphabet together.

(fold here)

Name: _____

You are your child's first and best teacher!

Here are ways to help your child practice skills while having fun!

Day 1 Say four letters of the alphabet and have your child tell which letter comes next. For example, *a, b, c, d, ? r, s, t, u, ?*

Day 2 Have your child name words that rhyme with *bug.*

Day 3 Look at a favorite picture book together. Ask your child to name the story characters and tell what they do.

Day 4 Your child is learning to use words that name shapes and sizes. Have your child find objects in your home that are big and objects that are square.

Day 5 Ask your child to introduce himself or herself to you, telling both name and address.

Read with your child EVERY DAY!

Alphabet Match

Directions

1. Look at the capital letter that begins each row.

2. Find its matching lowercase letter.

3. Color in that box.

F	a	e	g	f
M	m	n	r	a
Z	s	z	t	u
P	d	q	p	w
K	I	r	v	k

3

Name _____

Aa Bb Cc Dd Ee Ff Gg Hh Ii Jj Kk Ll Mm
Nn Oo Pp Qq Rr Ss Tt Uu Vv Ww Xx Yy Zz

 Write.

A a   B b   C c   D d

J j   K k   L l   M m

P p   Q q   R r   S s

Think Which letter comes before **N**?

 Directions: Trace the missing letters in the alphabet.

 Home Activity: Have your child say the letters of the alphabet in order.

Name _____

 Write. _____

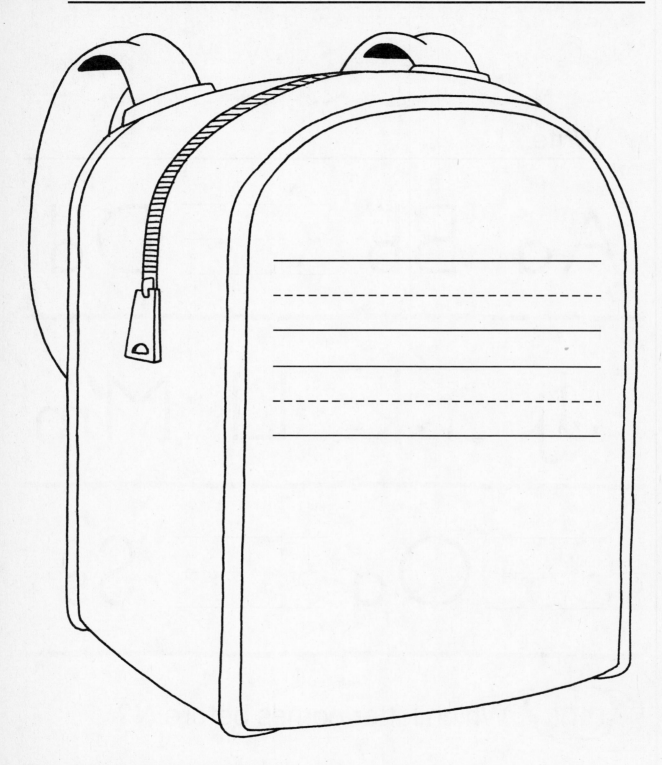

 Directions: Write your name on the backpack. Color the backpack.

 Home Activity: Ask your child to say a friend's full name.

Name _____

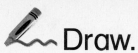 Draw.

 Directions: Draw your favorite character from the story and show what that character likes to do at school.

 Home Activity: Have your child tell about the drawing and what the character does to get ready for school.

Write.

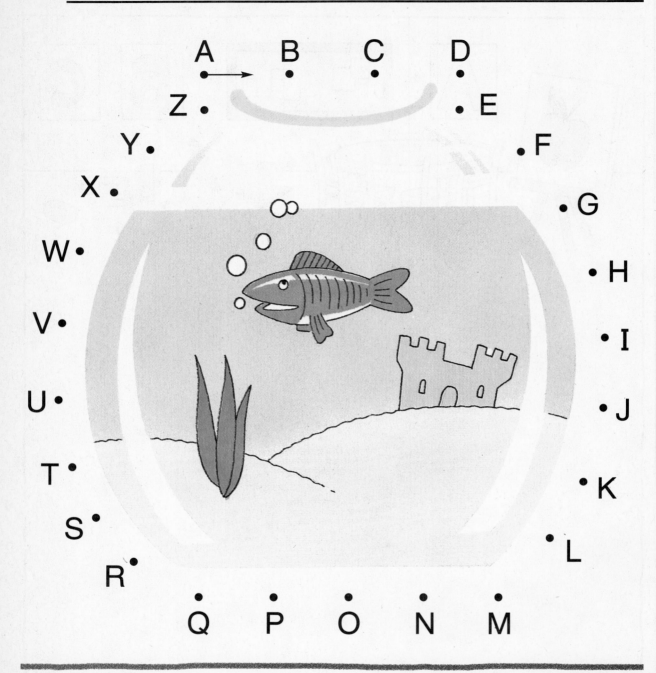

A → B C D

Z E

Y F

X G

W H

V I

U J

T K

S L

R Q P O N M

___

 **Think** Which letter comes after S?

 Directions: Draw lines to connect the letters A to Z in order.

 Home Activity: Ask your child to begin with a certain letter such as C and recite the remaining letters in order to Z.

6 Phonics: The Alphabet

Name _____

Draw.

Directions: What would you like to do in Miss Bindergarten's class? Draw a picture of yourself in Miss Bindergarten's class.

Home Activity: Ask your child to explain the picture.

Name _____

 Write.

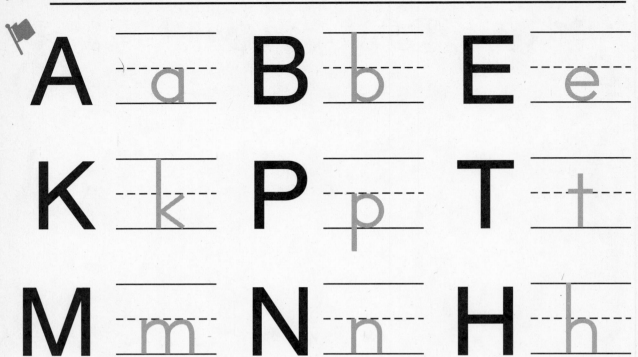

A a   B b   E e

K k   P p   T t

M m   N n   H h

 Draw a line.

P H N K Q W

B C D E F G

Y Q J E X F

 Directions: ⚑ Write and say the matching lowercase letter for each capital letter.
🦋 Draw a line under the row that shows some letters of the alphabet in order.

Family Times

Colors and Rhymes

It is the color of grass.
It is the color of grapes.
It rhymes with bean.
The color is green!

It is the color of the sky.
It is the color of a bird.
It rhymes with shoe.
The color is blue!

It is the color of a rose.
It is the color of a stop sign.
It rhymes with bed!
The color is red!

This rhyme shows pictures of rhyming words.
Recite "Colors and Rhymes" with your child.

(fold here)

Name: _____

You are your child's first and best teacher!

Here are ways to help your child practice skills while having fun!

Day 1 Help your child find the pictures of rhyming words on page 1.

Day 2 Help your child write the words ☐like☐ and ☐is☐ on a sheet of paper.

Day 3 Have your child retell a part of a favorite story.

Day 4 Have your child tell why a plate, fork, and spoon can go together.

Day 5 Help your child write his or her name on a sheet of paper.

Read with your child EVERY DAY!

Phonics Game:
Let's Help Cat

Cat wants to get to his mat.
How can you help Cat?

Game Directions

1. Look at the pictures.

2. Say the picture names.

3. Color the pictures that rhyme with **Cat.**

4. Follow the pictures you colored to show Cat the way to the mat.

2

3

Start

Draw a line.

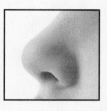

Draw a picture that rhymes with **red**.

 Directions: Draw lines to match the pictures with their rhyming names.

Home Activity: Have your child point to the matching pictures and say their names.

Phonics: Rhyme **11**

Name _____

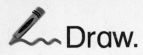 Draw.

 Write.

_____

- - - - - - - - - - - - - - - - - - -

_____

 Directions: Draw a picture and make up a name of an animal story character you like. Write the name on the line.

Home Activity: Talk about the animal's name with your child.

Name _____

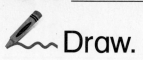Draw.

Directions: Use the colors on the page to draw something shown in *Cat's Colors*.

Home Activity: Have your child use the drawing to retell that part of the story.

Comprehension: Recall and Retell **13**

Draw a line.

Think Draw something that rhymes with ten.

 Directions: Look at and name the pictures. Draw a line under the pictures that rhyme with the one on the left.

 Home Activity: Ask your child to tell why each of the pictures was underlined.

14 Phonics: Rhyme

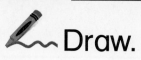 Draw.

 Directions: What was your favorite color in *Cat's Colors*? Draw something that color.

 Home Activity: Ask your child to tell you about the picture.

Name _____

Cat's Colors

Circle.

g	a	b	z	h	s
P	P	Q	L	C	D

Draw a line.

cat	is	my	like	is
is	a	like	by	like

Directions: Circle the letter that comes next in the alphabet. Name the first picture. Draw a line under the picture with a rhyming name. Draw a line under the words *like* and *is*.

16 Phonics: Assessment

© Scott Foresman K

Family Times

Come March with Me

March to the music. I can march.
Come march with me.
March to the music. I can march.
Come march with me.
I can march now. Come march with me.
I can march now. Come march with me.

This rhyme features words that begin with the *m* sound. Say "Come March with Me" with your child, while the two of you have fun marching around. The song can be sung to the tune of "Lil Liza Jane."

(fold here)

Name: _____

© Scott Foresman K

You are your child's first and best teacher!

Here are ways to help your child practice skills while having fun!

Day 1 Help your child find words in the song that rhyme and also begin with *m*.

Day 2 Have your child use the words *am* and *can* in sentences to tell about something that can be done.

Day 3 Have your child retell the order of events in a favorite story.

Day 4 Your child is learning about action words (verbs). Ask your child to show and tell you about things your child can do.

Day 5 Your child is learning to use words that tell about location (where), such as *top, middle, bottom, up,* and *down.* Name an item in your home and have your child tell its location.

Read with your child EVERY DAY!

Phonics Game:
M Words

Game Directions

1. Cut two plastic straws in half to make four pieces.

2. Name the following things:
an animal that begins with **m**
a food that begins with **m**
a place that begins with **m**
a word that tells something you do and begins with **m**

3. Each time you say an **m** word, place a piece of straw on one of the lines that make up the big **M**.

Answers:
moose, monkey, mule, mouse; milk; market; move; march

Mm

✏ <u>Circle.</u>

Think What letter do you
hear at the beginning of ?

_____

- - - - - - - -

Write the letter. _____

 Directions: *Moose* begins with the
letter *m*. Circle the pictures that begin
like *moose*.

 Home Activity: Have your child
name two things in your home that
begin like *moose*.

Draw a line.

 Directions: Draw lines to match each object with a child using that object. Tell about the action in each picture.

 Home Activity: Ask your child to tell you what happened in school today.

Draw a line.

 Directions: For each row draw a red line under the picture that comes first; blue, next; black, last.

 Home Activity: Ask your child to tell you the story of these three bears and their boat and the story about the pink pig.

Mm

✏️ Write.

[motorcycle] _____

_ _ _ _ _ _ _

_____

[map] _____

_ _ _ _ _ _ _

_____

[telephone] _____

_ _ _ _ _ _ _

_____

[mitten] _____

_ _ _ _ _ _ _

_____

[mop] _____

_ _ _ _ _ _ _

_____

[books] _____

_ _ _ _ _ _ _

_____

Think Choose a picture that begins with m. Use the word in a sentence.

 Directions: *Monkey* begins with the letter *m*. Write the letter *m* next to each picture that begins like *monkey*.

 Home Activity: Help your child choose a picture that begins with *m* and then write the letter *m*.

© Scott Foresman K

Name _____

✏️ Draw.

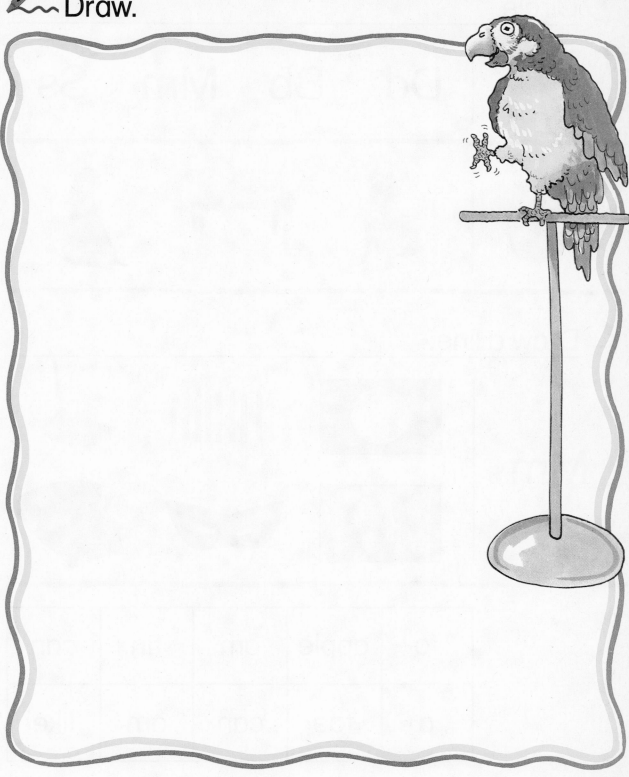

 Directions: Think of something that the parrot could ask you to do. Draw yourself doing what the parrot asks.

 Home Activity: Ask your child to tell you what happened at the end of the story *From Head to Toe*.

Name _____

 Circle.

  **Dd   Bb   Mm   Ss**

Draw a line.

Mm

to	apple	am	fin	can
a	toe	can	am	like

 Directions: Circle the letters that begin like the word *moose*. Name the pictures. Circle the picture that begins like *muffin*. Name the pictures. Draw a line under the pictures that begin with *m*. Draw a line under the words *am* and *can*.

24   Phonics: Assessment

© Scott Foresman K

1

Family Times

Hi, My Name Is Rita

Hi, my name is Rita. I have fun.
I like to roller-skate. I like to run.
When I ride my bike, I like it best.
I ride all day and then I rest.

Hi, my name is Rita. Watch me row.
I have a red boat. Watch me go!
When it starts to rain, I'll rush away.
I'll row again another day.

This rhyme features words that begin with *r*. Recite "Hi, My Name Is Rita" with your child.

(fold here)

Name: _____

You are your child's first and best teacher!

Here are ways to help your child practice skills while having fun!

Day 1 Help your child find words in the poem on page 1 that begin with *r*.

Day 2 Have your child use the words *red* and *blue* in sentences. Print one of the sentences and ask your child to find and read the word *red* or *blue*.

Day 3 Point to or show a pair of shoes, a jacket, and a hat, or choose three other clothing items. Ask your child to tell how these things are alike and how they are different.

Day 4 Your child is learning color words. Ask your child to use color words to describe two objects in your home.

Day 5 Your child is learning about words that name things, (nouns). Ask your child to tell you words that name things in your kitchen and other rooms in your home.

Read with your child EVERY DAY!

Let's Go to the Party

Game Directions

Play with a partner.

1. Use 1 penny and 2 markers.

2. Take turns tossing a coin.
   If the coin shows
   move one space.

   If the coin shows
   move two spaces.

3. When a marker lands on **r**, the player says a word
   that begins with the same sound as **red**. If you do
   not land on the letter **r**, your partner takes a turn.

4. The first player to the party wins.

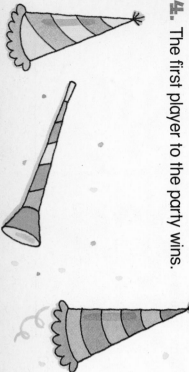

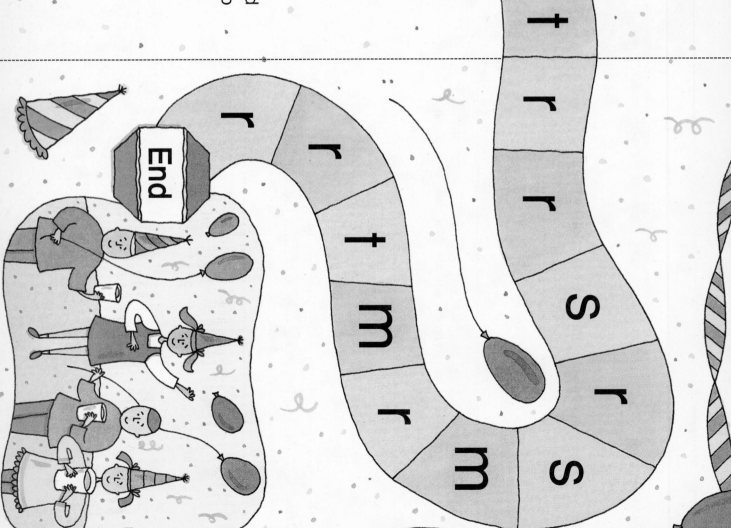

Start

t

r

r

s

r

s

m

r

m

t

r

t

r

End

2

3

Name _____

Rr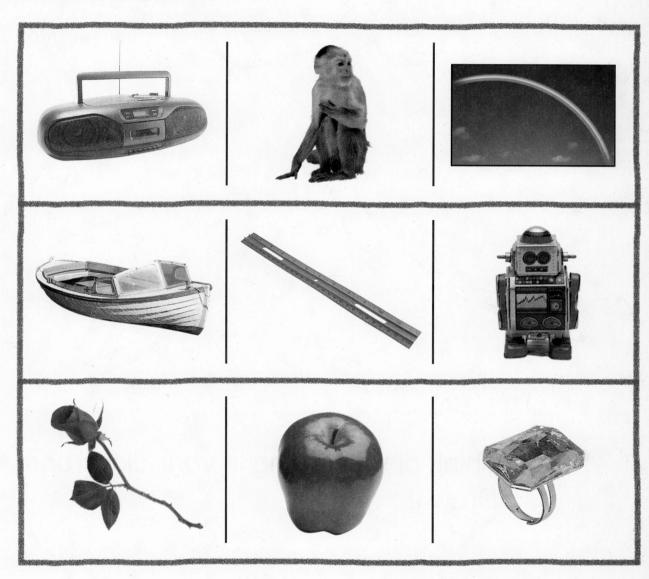

✎ Draw a line.

✎ Write the letters Rr.

 Directions: Point to the rabbit. *Rabbit* begins with *r*. Name the pictures. Draw a line under the pictures that begin with *r*.

 Home Activity: Have your child name pictures that begin with *r* on this page.

Name _____

Color.

Think of something in your classroom.
Draw it.

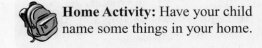

Home Activity: Have your child name some things in your home.

© Scott Foresman   K

Name _____

 Circle.

 Directions: Look at the pictures in each row. Circle the picture that is different. Tell how it is different.

 Home Activity: Have your child tell you about the pictures that are alike in each row.

© Scott Foresman K

Comprehension: Compare and Contrast 29

Name _____

R r

✏️ Write. _____

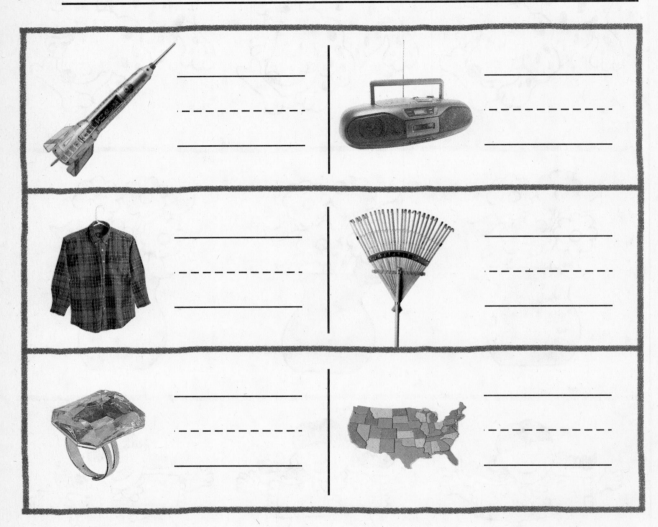

☁️ **Think** Draw something that begins with **r**.

 Directions: Name the pictures. Write the letters *Rr* next to the pictures that begin like *rug*.

 Home Activity: Have your child practice writing the letters *Rr* on paper.

Name _____

✎ Draw.

 Directions: Draw a picture of yourself at the party. Tell what you are wearing. How is it different from clothes in the story?

 Home Activity: Ask your child to talk about the drawing.

Circle.

Dd   Rr   Mm   Ss

 |

	Mm Rr Aa	Mm Rr Aa
	Mm Rr Aa	 Mm Rr Aa

 Draw a line.

and	red	like	but	blue
blue	is	a	red	but

 Directions: 🚩 Circle the letters that begin the word *rope*. 🦋 Name the pictures. Circle the pictures that begin like *ring*. 🔑 Circle the letter *r* if the picture name begins like *robot*. 🌼 Draw a line under the words *blue* and *red*.

Family Times

All on a Summer Sunday

I see a sailboat in the sea.
I see a surfer in the sea.
I see a sea lion in the sea.
All on a summer Sunday.

I see a softball. Play with me.
I see a seesaw. Play with me.
I see a sandbox. Play with me.
All on a summer Sunday.

This rhyme features words that begin with *s*. Recite "All on a Summer Sunday" with your child.

(fold here)

Name: _____

You are your child's first and best teacher!

Here are ways to help your child practice skills while having fun!

Day 1　Help your child find words in the rhyme on page 1 that begin with *s*.

Day 2　Have your child name some words that begin with *s*.

Day 3　Look at a favorite storybook together and ask your child to name the characters in the story.

Day 4　Ask your child why these words can go together: *tiger, elephant, gorilla.* Continue with other groups of words as long as you both enjoy the game.

Day 5　Ask your child to name some people in your home, such as Mom, Dad, Grandma, and so on.

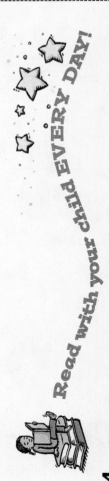

Read with your child EVERY DAY!

4

Phonics Game: S Words

Game Directions

1. Use 6 pennies or markers.

2. Choose an item to buy. You can only buy things whose names begin with the letter **s**.

3. Put a penny or marker on the item you want to buy.

4. Name all the things you have bought at the sale.

Sale

Name _____

Ss

✏️ Draw a line.

✏️ Write the letters Ss.

 Directions: Draw a line from the pictures that begin with *Ss* to the suitcase. Draw one more thing that begins with *s* inside.

 Home Activity: Have your child name the *s* pictures on this page.

Name _____

 Color.

Directions: Draw one more person in each picture. Color. Tell about the pictures using words that name people and what they do.

 Home Activity: Have your child name the people in your home.

Name _____

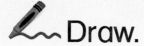 Draw.

 Directions: Draw a picture to show how the cats feel at the end of the story.

 Home Activity: Ask your child to tell you what the story *Ginger* is about.

Comprehension: Character **37**

Name _____

Ss

✏️ Write.

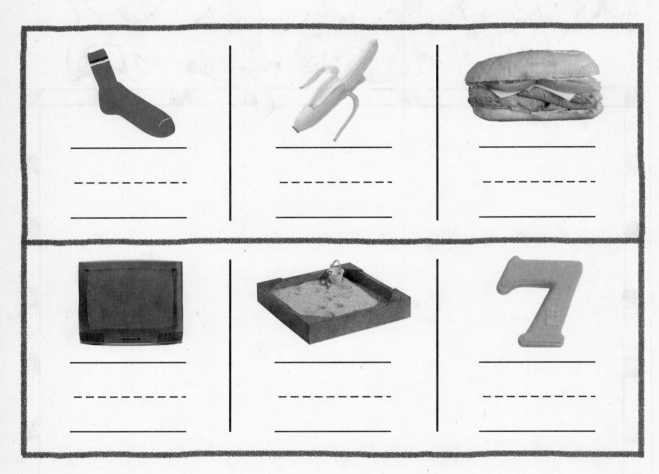

Think Which word rhymes with rock
and is something you wear?

_____

_____

 **Directions:** Name the pictures. Then
write the letters *Ss* if the picture
begins like *sun*.

🎒 **Home Activity:** Say three words, such as
silly, *Willie*, and *hilly*. Ask your child
which begins with the same sound as *sun*.

© Scott Foresman K

Name _____

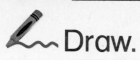

 Draw.

 Directions: Draw a picture to show what you would do to take care of them if Ginger and the kitten were your pets.

 Home Activity: Talk with your child about how to take care of a pet.

Name _____

 Draw a line.

 | **Rr** **Bb** **Aa** **Ss**

  |

 Circle.

Ss

 Write.

Ss

_____   _____   _____

- - - - - - - - -   - - - - - - - - -   - - - - - - - - -

_____   _____   _____

Directions: Draw a line under the letters that begin the word *sailboat*. Name the pictures. Underline the pictures that begin like *sandwich*. Circle the pictures that begin with *s*. Write capital and lowercase *Ss* on the lines.

40 Phonics: Assessment

Family Times

Make a Stew

Make a stew, make a stew, make it nice.
Meatballs, spinach, and some rice.
Mix it and stir it and roast it too.
Serve it with a salad for me and you!

This rhyme features words that begin with *m*, *r*, or *s*. Recite "Make a Stew" with your child. Talk about the things you use to make a stew.

(fold here)

Name: _____

You are your child's first and best teacher!

Here are ways to help your child practice skills while having fun!

Day 1 Help your child find words in the rhyme on page 1 that begin with the letters *m*, *r*, and *s*.

Day 2 Read a story together. Have your child point out the words on a page that begin with the letters *m*, *r*, and *s*.

Day 3 Have your child tell about the characters in a favorite story.

Day 4 Your child is learning number words, such as *one*, *two*, *three*. Encourage your child to look for number words on packages and labels at home and at stores. When you see a number word, point to it and help your child read the word.

Day 5 Have your child use sentences to tell about what happened in school today.

Read with your child EVERY DAY!

Phonics Game: Three in a Row

Materials You each need a different colored pencil or crayon.

Game Directions

Play with a partner.

1. Choose a picture. Name it. Write the letter that begins the name.

2. Now your partner takes a turn.

3. The player who gets three across ⟷ , down ↓, up ↑, or this way ↗, says, "Three in a row."

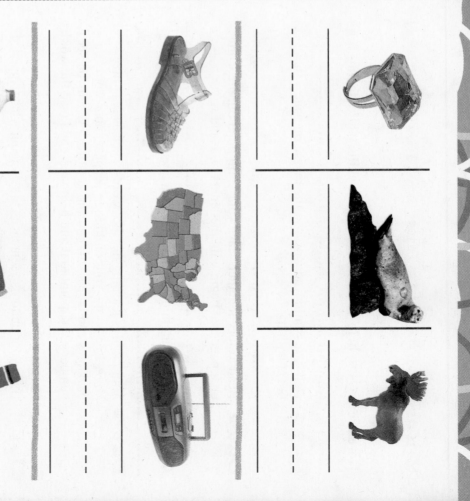

Name _____

M m  R r  S s

 Color.

 **Mm**

 Rr

 **Ss**

 Write the letters.

_____   _____   _____

- - - - - - - - - - -   - - - - - - - - - - -   - - - - - - - - - - -

_____   _____   _____

 Directions: Color the pictures in each row that begin with the same letters as the object on the left. Write *Mm*, *Rr*, and *Ss*.

Home Activity: Help your child make a sign, such as *socks* for a sock drawer, using one of the letters learned this week.

Name _____

 Draw a line.

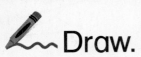

 Draw.

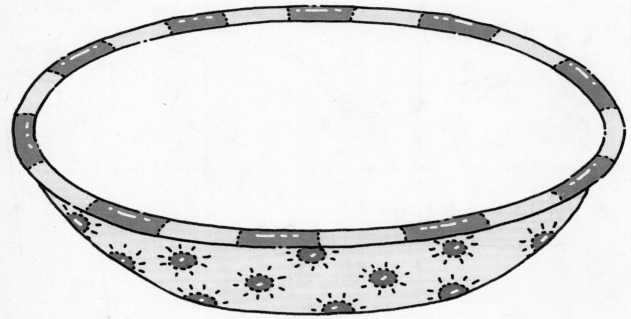

 Directions: Draw lines to put foods together. Draw a food that could go in the bowl.

Home Activity: Tell about what you drew in the bowl.

Name _____

✏️ ～Draw.

 Directions: Draw a character from *Mama Provi and the Pot of Rice* preparing one of the foods at the top of the page.

 Home Activity: Ask your child to tell about the person in the picture. Ask, *What is the person doing?*

Comprehension: Character **45**

Mm  Rr  Ss

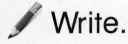 Write.

_____
- - - - - - - - - - -

_____
- - - - - - - - - - -

Think Use mouse, sat, and rocket in a sentence.

 Directions: Name the pictures. Write the upper and lowercase letters that begin each picture name.

 Home Activity: Have your child look for the letters *Rr*, *Ss*, and *Mm* in books or magazines in your home.

Panel 8

Y is for ⬤ .

_____

_ _ _ _ _ _

_____ is for  .

8

(fold here)

Panel 1

My Little Book

This ABC book belongs to

_____

_____

_____

_____

_____

Directions: Write your name.

1

✂ (cut here)

Panel 6

Q is for 👑 .

_____

_ _ _ _ _ _

_____ is for 🍴 .

_____

_ _ _ _ _ _

_____ is for 🥪 .

T is for ⛺ .

© Scott Foresman K

6

Panel 3

E is for 🐘 .

F is for 🚧 .

G is for 🚪 .

_____

_ _ _ _ _ _

_____ is for  .

3

A is for  .

B is for .

C is for .

_____
- - - - - -
_____ is for .

Directions: Write the missing capital letter.

②

U is for .

_____
- - - - - - - -
_____ is for .

_____
- - - - - - - -
_____ is for .

X is for .

⑦

I is for .

J is for .

K is for .

_____
- - - - - -
_____ is for .

④

_____
- - - - - - -
_____ is for .

N is for .

O is for .

_____
- - - - - - -
_____ is for .

⑤

© Scott Foresman K

Name _____

✍ Draw.

 Directions: Pretend you are Lucy in the story. How do you feel about being sick? Draw something that would cheer you up.

 Home Activity: Ask your child to tell you about the picture.

Draw a line.

	Mm Ss Rr		Mm Ss Rr		Mm Ss Rr
	Mm Ss Rr		Mm Ss Rr		Mm Ss Rr

 Circle.

	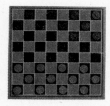		

 Directions: Name the picture in each box. Draw a line under the letters that begin that word. Name the first picture in each row. Circle the picture that begins with the same sound as the first picture.

© Scott Foresman K

Family Times

Busy Animals

Busy bunny likes to bounce.
Bounce like a bunny.
Bounce, bounce, bounce.

Busy beagle likes to bark.
Bark like a beagle.
Bark, bark, bark.

Busy bumblebee likes to buzz.
Buzz like a bumblebee.
Buzz, buzz, buzz.

This rhyme features words that begin with *b*. Recite "Busy Animals" with your child.

(fold here)

Name: _____

You are your child's first and best teacher!

Here are ways to help your child practice skills while having fun!

Day 1 Help your child find words in the rhyme on page 1 that begin with *b*.

Day 2 Write the words *but* and *I* on a piece of paper. Have your child read the words. Use each word in a sentence.

Day 3 Have your child look at pictures in a favorite story and tell how the pictures help tell the story.

Day 4 Your child is learning to share ideas. Read a book with your child, then share ideas about it. Ask, "What part did you like?"

Day 5 Ask your child to tell you words that name people, places, and things.

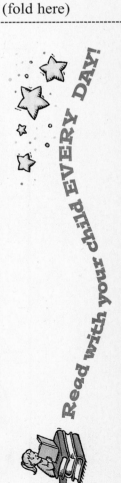

Read with your child EVERY DAY!

Phonics Game: B Words

Game Directions

1. Use 8 pennies or markers.

2. Choose a picture from the game board and say its name.

3. Put a marker on the picture if its name begins with **b**.

4. When you have marked three pictures across or down, say, "B words."

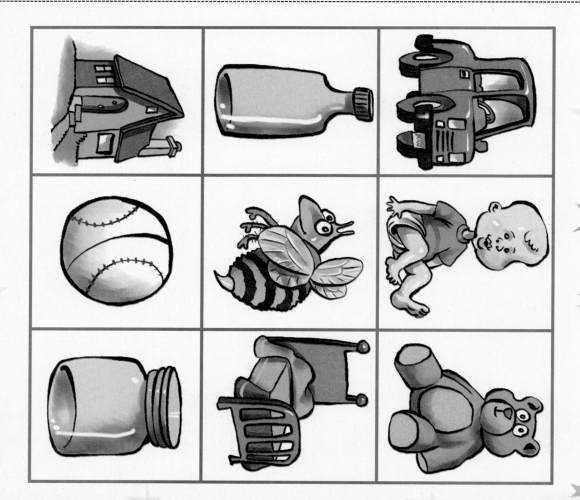

Bb

Draw a line.

© Scott Foresman K

Think Write the letters **Bb**. _ _ _ _ _ _ _

 Directions: Draw a line to the box from each toy whose name begins with *b*. Draw another toy that begins with *b*.

 Home Activity: Have your child name two things in your home that begin like *bear*.

Name _____

 Circle.   Draw a line.

Directions: Circle the pictures that name places and draw a line under the pictures that name people.

Home Activity: Have your child point to the pictures that name things that are not places or people.

✏️ Draw.

 Directions: Draw a picture to show what the mouse might do next.

 Home Activity: Ask your child to tell a story about the mouse in the picture.

Comprehension: Using Illustrations **55**

Name _____

Bb

🖉 Write.

© Scott Foresman K

Think Name a word that rhymes
with **rug** and begins with **b**.

 Directions: Name the pictures. Write
Bb if the picture begins like *ball*.

 **Home Activity:** Ask your child to name
the *b* words on this page.

56 Phonics: Consonant *Bb*

Name _____

✎ Draw.

 Directions: Invent your own animal and draw its picture. Tell a partner your animal's name and the noise it makes.

 Home Activity: Help your child write the invented animal's name.

Name _____

 Circle.

Dd Bb Aa Cc

Bb

 Draw a line.

am	I	see	and	I
like	see	and	but	like

 Directions: ⚑ Circle the letters that stand for the beginning sound in *bat*. 🦋 Circle the pictures whose names begin like *bear*. ⚷ Circle the pictures whose names begin with *Bb*. 🌼 Draw a line under the word *I* using a red crayon and under the word *but* using a blue crayon.

Family Times

Two Fat Turkeys

Two fat turkeys are we.
We talk and sit by a tree.
When two toads come,
We start to run.
Two fat turkeys are we!

Two tiny toads are we.
We tiptoe to a tree.
When two turkeys run,
We talk and have fun.
Two tiny toads are we!

This rhyme features words that begin or end with *t*.
Recite or sing "Two Fat Turkeys" with your child.

(fold here)

Name: _____

You are your child's first and best teacher!

Here are ways to help your child practice skills while having fun!

Day 1 Help your child find words in the rhyme on page 1 that begin with the letter *t*.

Day 2 Help your child find words in the rhyme on page 1 that end with the letter *t*.

Day 3 Ask your child to say three words that begin with *t*.

Day 4 Ask your child to say words that name more than one thing, such as *toes*.

Day 5 Have your child look at pictures in a favorite book and tell who the characters are.

Read with your child EVERY DAY!

Phonics Activity: T Words

Activity Directions

1. Say the picture names.
2. Color the pictures that **begin** with **t** red.
3. Color pictures that **end** with **t** blue.

2

2 3

Name _____

T t

 Draw a line. _____

Think Draw a picture of something that ends with t on the table.

 **Directions:** Say the name of each picture. Draw a line from each picture that begins with *t* to the table.

 Home Activity: Have your child name two things in your home that begin like *top*.

© Scott Foresman K

Phonics: Consonant *Tt* **61**

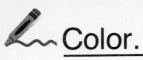

Name _____

✏️ Color.

 Directions: Color the pictures that show more than one animal in a fenced in area.

 Home Activity: Have your child tell you how many of each animal were colored.

62 Grammar: More Than One (Plural Nouns)

Draw.

Directions: Draw some characters who come to eat at the restaurant in *Dinner at the Panda Palace.*

Home Activity: Ask your child to name the animals that were drawn and tell what they were doing before dinner.

Comprehension: Character **63**

Name _____

Tt

🖊 Write.

Think

Make up a sentence with Tom, tell, and table.

 Directions: Name the pictures. Write *Tt* if the picture begins like *turkey*.

 Home Activity: Have your child use a finger to trace over the letters on the page.

Name _____

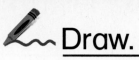

 Draw. _____

 Directions: Pretend that you have lunch with some animals from the story. Draw what you would eat on the plate.

 Home Activity: Ask your child to tell about the food the animals ate.

© Scott Foresman K

Circle.

  **Ss   Bb   Tt   Mm   Rr**

Draw a line.

Tt

Directions: Circle the letters that begin the word *turkey*. Circle the pictures whose names begin like *toad*. Circle the pictures whose names end like *nut*. Name the pictures. Draw a line under the pictures that begin with *Tt*.

Family Times

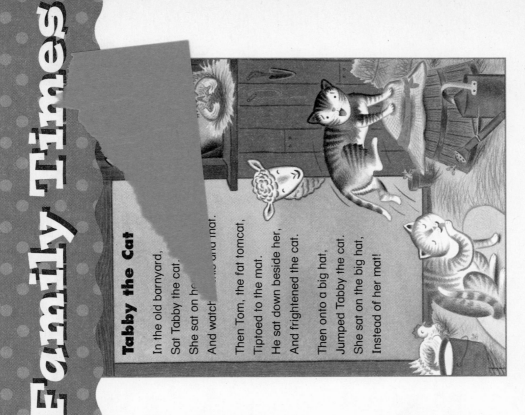

Tabby the Cat

In the old barnyard,
Sat Tabby the cat.
She sat on h...
And watch... ... and ...

Then Tom, the fat tomcat,
Tiptoed to the mat.
He sat down beside her,
And frightened the cat.

Then onto a big hat,
Jumped Tabby the cat.
She sat on the big hat,
Instead of her mat!

This rhyme features words that have the short *a* sound. Recite or sing "Tabby the Cat" with your child.

(fold here)

Name: _____

You are your child's first and best teacher!

Here are ways to help your child practice skills while having fun!

Day 1 Help your child find words in the rhyme on page 1 that rhyme with *cat*.

Day 2 Write the words *go* and *the* on a sheet of paper. Help your child find these words in books you read together.

Day 3 Read a favorite story and then have your child retell the story.

Day 4 Your child is learning to listen and share ideas in order to solve problems. Share a problem with your child, such as, "The socks are clean and dry. What should we do with them next?"

Day 5 Ask your child to tell you a sentence about a person, place, or thing.

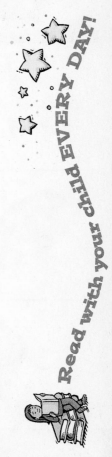

Read with your child EVERY DAY!

Phonics Game: Short a Words

Game Directions

1. Use 6 pennies.

2. Choose a picture and say its name.

3. If the picture's name has the short a sound as in cat, put a penny on it.

4. When you have put down 6 pennies, say, "apple."

a

 Draw a line.

 Directions: Draw a line from the picture with the short *a* sound as in *mat* to the mat. Draw a picture of another *a* word.

 Home Activity: Have your child name two things in your home that have the short *a* sound.

✏ Circle.

 Directions: Use crayons to circle the people in blue, the places in green, and the things in red.

 Home Activity: Have your child tell you about each person, place, and thing that was circled.

✏ **Draw.**

© Scott Foresman K

 Directions: Recall the story *No, No, Titus!* Draw a picture that tells something about the story.

Home Activity: Ask your child to tell you about the picture.

Name _____

Aa  a

✏️ Write.

💭 Think   Name an animal that begins like **apple**.

 Directions: Name the pictures. Write the letter *a* next to each picture that has the short *a* sound as in *apple* and *can*.

 Home Activity: Have your child trace over the letters with a pencil.

© Scott Foresman K

72 Phonics: Short *a*

Name _____

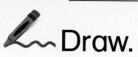 Draw.

 Directions: What would you do with Titus, if Titus were your dog? Draw a picture.

 Home Activity: Ask your child to tell you what the dog in the picture is doing.

Name _____

 Circle.

 | r s a b

 |

 Draw a line.

Aa |

go	but	the	go	is

© Scott Foresman K

 Directions: Circle the letter that stands for the short *a* sound as in *cat*. Circle the pictures that have the short *a* sound as in *hat*. Draw a line under the pictures that have the short *a* sound. Draw a line under the words *go* and *the*.

Family Times

Fun, Fun with My Friends

Oh, give me a home,
Where the foxes can roam,
And the fawn and the fishes can play.
Where field mice can run,
And the fools can have fun.
And my friends can roam free every day.

Fun, fun with my friends.
Where the fawn and the fishes can play.
Where field mice can run,
And the foals can have fun.
And my friends can roam free every day.

This rhyme features words that begin with *f*. Sing "Fun, Fun with My Friends" to the tune of "Home, Home on the Range" with your child. Then ask your child to name the pictures that begin with *f*.

(fold here)

Name: _____

You are your child's first and best teacher!

Here are ways to help your child practice skills while having fun!

Day 1 Help your child find words in the rhyme on page 1 that begin with *f*.

Day 2 Read a favorite story or poem together. Have your child listen for words that begin the same as *fun*.

Day 3 Read a book together. Then ask your child to tell you where and when the story takes place.

Day 4 Your child is learning to be a polite speaker. Ask your child to speak slowly and clearly and tell you about something fun that happened in school today.

Day 5 Ask your child to pantomime some actions that take place in the kitchen, such as mixing, cooking, cutting. Have your child name an action word (verb) that describes each activity.

Read with your child EVERY DAY!

Phonics Game: Picture Search

Game Directions

1. Look at the picture and color it.

2. Name the things you see.

3. Then use a black crayon to circle the things that begin with f.

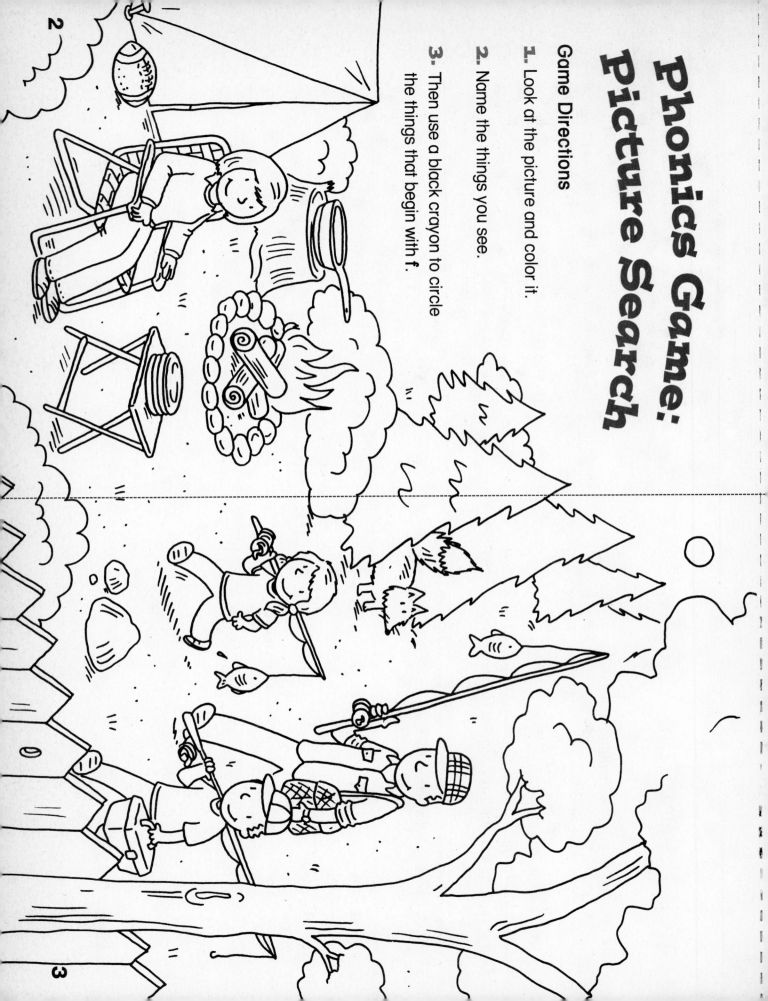

2
3

Ff

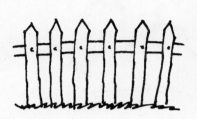 Color. _____

Write the letters Ff. ---------

 Directions: Color the pictures that begin like *fish*. Then write the letters *Ff*.

 Home Activity: Have your child name all the pictures that were colored on this page.

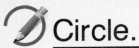 Circle.

 Directions: Circle the pictures that show an action.

 Home Activity: Have your child name action words shown in the pictures on this page.

Name _____

✏ Draw.

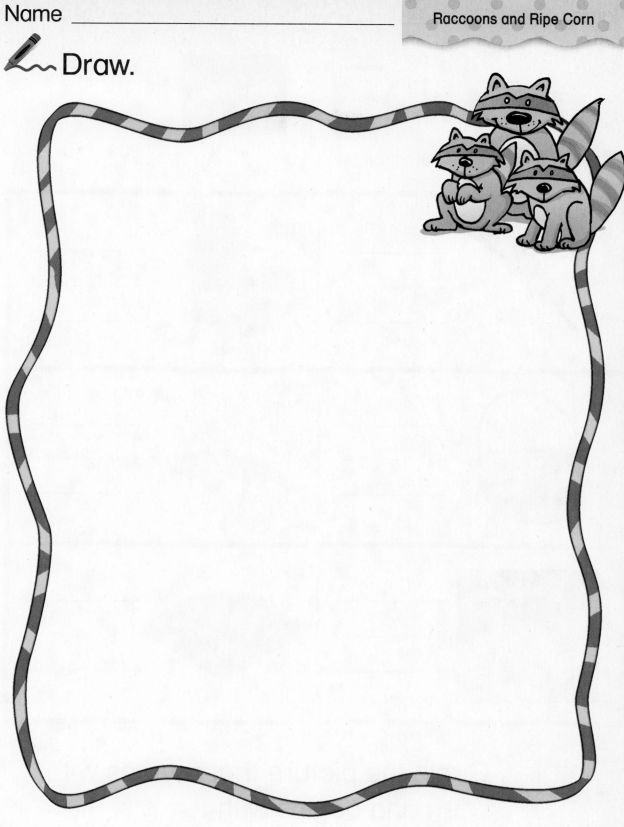

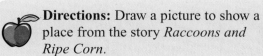 **Directions:** Draw a picture to show a place from the story *Raccoons and Ripe Corn*.

 Home Activity: Ask your child to tell about the place and what happens there.

Comprehension: Story Elements **79**

Name _____

Ff

✏️ Write.

(Think) **Circle the picture that rhymes with wish and begins with f.**

 Directions: Name the pictures. Write *Ff* if the name begins like *fox*.

 **Home Activity:** Have your child practice writing capital *F* and lowercase *f* on a separate sheet of paper.

© Scott Foresman K

80 Phonics: Consonant *Ff*

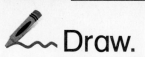Draw.

 Directions: Draw a picture to show a new ending for the story *Raccoons and Ripe Corn*.

 Home Activity: Ask your child to tell you the story with the new ending.

Name _____

 Circle.

Tt Ff Bb Ss

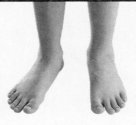 Draw a line.

Ff

 Directions: Circle the letters that begin the word *fish*.  Name the pictures. Circle the pictures that begin like *feather*. Draw a line under the pictures that begin with *f*.

82 Phonics: Assessment

© Scott Foresman K

Family Times

Nan the Nanny Goat

Nan the nanny goat has some fun,
Has some fun, has some fun.
Nan the nanny goat has some fun,
And likes to nap at noon.

Nan the nanny goat eats the nuts,
Eats the nuts, eats the nuts.
Nan the nanny goat eats the nuts,
And likes to nap at noon.

This rhyme features words that begin with *n*. Recite "Nan the Nanny Goat" with your child.

(fold here)

Name: _____

You are your child's first and best teacher!

Here are ways to help your child practice skills while having fun!

Day 1 Help your child find words in the rhyme on page 1 that begin with *n*.

Day 2 Your child is learning to identify new words. Write the words *it* and *have*. Ask your child to read the words and make up a sentence that uses each word.

Day 3 Ask your child to look at a favorite storybook and retell the story to you.

Day 4 Your child is learning to listen to ideas. Show your child a photograph from a newspaper or magazine. Have your child listen as you share ideas about the photograph. Then have your child share ideas about the photo while you listen.

Day 5 Ask your child to say words that tell things he or she can do, such as read, sleep, talk, and sing.

Read with your child EVERY DAY!

Phonics Game: N Words

Game Directions

1. Find N or n in the picture.

2. Color each part of the picture with N or n brown.

3. You will find something that a bird makes. What is it?

4. Finish coloring the picture.

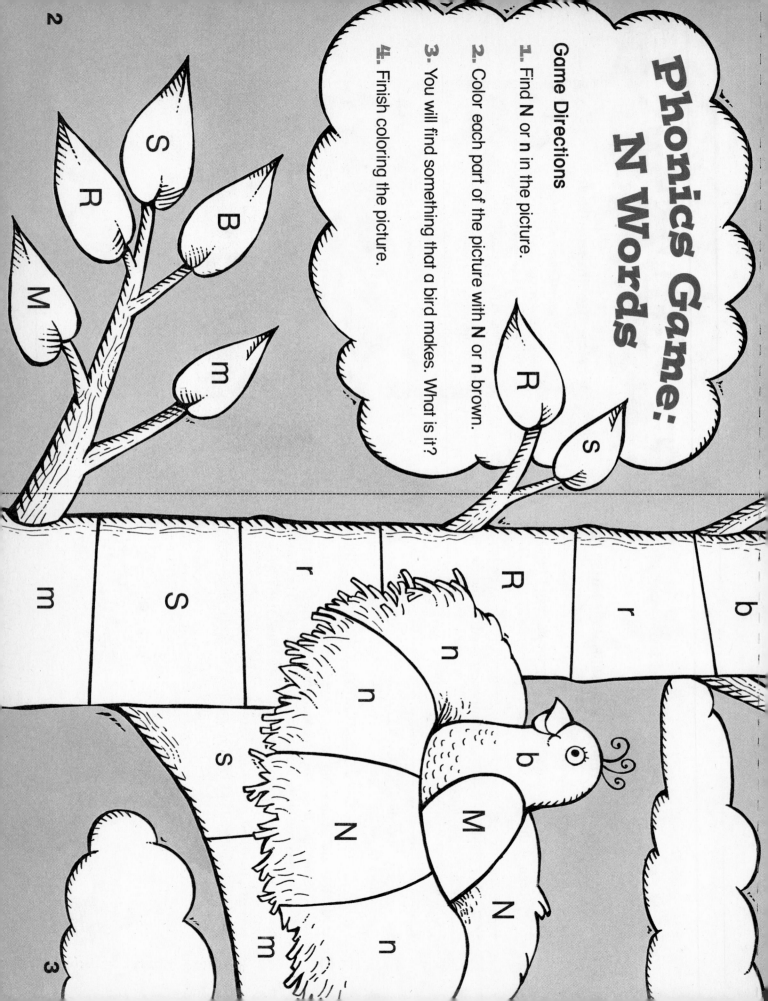

Name _____

Nn

✐ Circle.

✐ Write the letters Nn. _____

 Directions: Circle the things in the picture that begin with *Nn*. Then write the letters *Nn*.

 Home Activity: Have your child name two things in your home that begin with the same sound as *number*.

Phonics: Consonant *Nn* **85**

Circle.

 Directions: Circle the pictures that show what people can do and tell what the action is.

 Home Activity: Have your child show you an action (such as jump, dance, hop) and tell what the action is.

Name _____

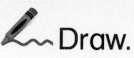 Draw.

 Directions: Choose an animal from the story *Time to Sleep*. Draw a picture to show where it sleeps for winter.

 Home Activity: Ask your child to tell what some animals do to get ready for winter.

Comprehension: Recall and Retell **87**

Name _____

Nn

✏️ Write.

Think Make up sentences with these words:
Nan, nurse, and nap.

 Directions: Name each picture. Write capital *N* if the picture begins with *n*, lowercase *n* if it ends with *n*.

 Home Activity: Have your child say the name of each picture and tell if it begins or ends with *n*.

88 Phonics: Consonant *Nn*

Name _____

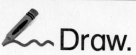Draw.

Directions: Draw pictures to show what Bear might dream of when she goes into her cave for a long winter sleep.

Home Activity: Ask your child to tell you when Bear will wake up and what it might be like outside then.

Reader Response **89**

Draw a line.

 |  **Mm Bb Dd Nn Cc**

  |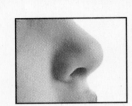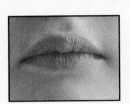

 Circle.

 Nn |

have	it	like	red	it

 Directions: Draw a line under the letters that stand for the sound at the beginning of the word *nest*.  Draw a line under the pictures that begin like *nut*. Circle the pictures that end with *n*. Circle the words *have* and *it*.

Family Times

Now What Do You Think of That?

"I really like this mat,"
Said Pat the furry cat.
"I really like a mat that's big."
Now what do you think of that?

The mouse ran to the mat,
And sat beside the cat.
The mouse said, "I like your big mat."
Now what do you think of that?

The skunk ran to the mat,
And sat beside the cat.
The cat and mouse began to run.
Now what do you think of that?

This rhyme features words that end with *at*. Recite "Now What Do You Think of That?" with your child and ask what the mouse and cat did after the skunk came.

(fold here)

Name: _____

You are your child's first and best teacher!

Here are ways to help your child practice skills while having fun!

Day 1 Help your child find words in the rhyme on page 1 that rhyme with *bat*.

Day 2 Write the words *do* and *not* on a sheet of paper. Have your child read the words and use them in sentences.

Day 3 Read aloud or tell a make-believe story. Have your child retell the story to you. Ask your child what makes the story make believe.

Day 4 Your child is learning to be a good listener. Listen as your child tells you about something that happened at school today. Then share something that happened in your day and have your child listen carefully to you.

Day 5 Ask your child to name action words (verbs), that tell about something fun to do.

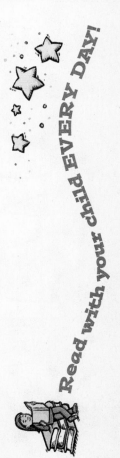

Read with your child EVERY DAY!

Phonics Game: Picture Search

Game Directions

1. Look at the picture.

2. Think about what is happening.

3. Then draw an X on these things:
   feather, bench, sandwich, radio, mug, nuts.

Name _____

✏️ **Circle.**

Bb Rr Ss

Nn Rr Tt

Dd Mm Bb

Ff Mm Ss

Ff Nn Bb

Nn Bb Rr

Mm Ss Tt

Rr Ff Nn

Ss Ff Tt

Think What letter is at the end of  ?

 Directions: Name each picture. Circle the capital and lowercase letters that begin the picture name.

 Home Activity: Have your child name each picture and say its beginning letter sound.

Name _____

 Circle.

The dogs run.

The girls jump.

The boys ride.

 Directions: Listen to the sentence about each picture. Circle and write the action word.

 Home Activity: Have your child use the word *play* in a sentence.

© Scott Foresman K

Name _____

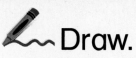Draw.

 Directions: Draw a picture showing the place where the family in *Looking for Crabs* went.

 Home Activity: Ask your child to use the picture to retell the story *Looking for Crabs*.

Name _____

 Write.

_____ _____

_____ _____

Think Write a word that begins with S

and rhymes with **hat.** _____

 Directions: Name each picture. Write the capital and lowercase letter that begins each picture.

 Home Activity: Have your child name three things (such as *bat, map, bag*) that have the short *a* sound.

© Scott Foresman K

96 Phonics: Skill Review

My Little Book

This book belongs to

_____

- - - - - - - - - - - -

Directions: Write your name.

✂ (cut here)

1

I see a ____ an.

(fold here)

3

_____

- - - - - - - - - - - -

_____

Directions: Say the picture names.
Write the letter that ends each name.

© Scott Foresman K

8

Directions: Draw a picture of something that rhymes with **pan**.

6

I see a ____ ap.

Directions: Say the picture name.
Write the letter that begins the name.

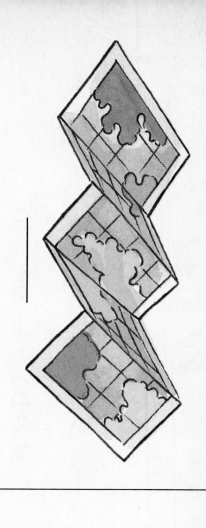

Directions: Draw a picture of something that rhymes with **cat**.

I see a ____ andbox.

I see a ____ aby.

Name _____

 Draw.

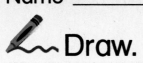

 Directions: Draw a picture of a new hiding place for a hermit crab. Tell how you think the crab feels now.

 Home Activity: Ask your child to tell you about the picture and why it is a good hiding place.

Name _____

 Draw a line.

 |

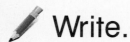

like	can	not	do	but

Write.

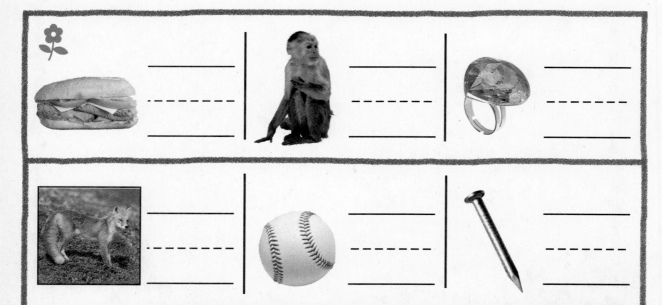

 Directions: 🚩 Draw a line under the picture that rhymes with *cat*. 🦋 Draw a line under the picture that begins like *tiger*. 🔑 Draw a line under the words *do* and *not*. 🌸 Write the letter that begins each picture name.

100 Phonics: Assessment

Family Times

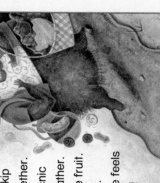

Patty

Patty loves to put a pen
And paper in her pocket.
Patty loves to put a picture
In her lovely locket.

Patty loves to pack her purse
With pennies and a nickel.
Patty loves to pack her purse
With peanuts and a pickle!

Patty loves to hop and skip
And clap her hands together.
Patty loves to have a picnic
When there's sunny weather.

Patty packs some purple fruit.
Patty packs a pork chop.
Patty packs up when she feels
The patter of a raindrop!

This rhyme features words that begin or end with *p*. Read "Patty" with your child and act out the rhyme together

(fold here)

Name: _____

You are your child's first and best teacher!

Here are ways to help your child practice skills while having fun!

Day 1 Help your child find words in the rhyme on page 1 that begin with *p*.

Day 2 Help your child find words in the rhyme on page 1 that end with *p*.

Day 3 Read the last line of the rhyme on page 1 with your child and talk about what causes Patty to pack up.

Day 4 Your child is learning to listen to a story for enjoyment. Read a funny story to your child, then talk about the funny parts.

Day 5 Your child is learning to make sentences. Ask your child to use sentences to tell you what a favorite toy looks like.

Read with your child EVERY DAY!

Phonics Activity: P Animals

Activity Directions

1. Choose an animal and say its name.

2. Write p on the picture if the animal's name begins with p.

3. Put an X on the picture if the animal's name does not begin with p.

4. Let's have a party for the animals. Draw a  on each animal that begins with p.

3

Name _____

P p

Draw a line.

Write the letters **P p**.

 Directions: Draw a line from the basket to each picture that begins like *picnic*. Draw another food that begins with *p*.

 Home Activity: Have your child name two things in your home that begin like *picnic*.

Color.

 Directions: Color the pictures that show something about the poem "Mary's Lamb." Tell why you colored each picture.

 Home Activity: Have your child tell about the poem by finishing this sentence: *One day a lamb . . .*

Name _____

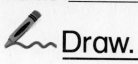Draw.

 Directions: Show how Lilly felt after Mr. Slinger took away her purse.

 Home Activity: Ask your child to explain what things happened in *Lilly's Purple Plastic Purse* and why they happened.

Comprehension: Cause and Effect **105**

Name _____

 Circle.

Nn ⟨Pp⟩ Rr

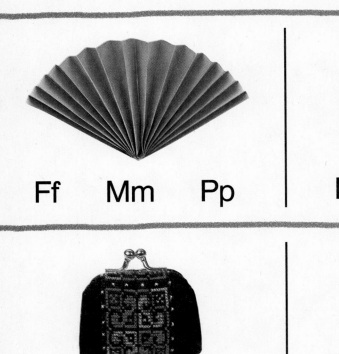

Ff   Mm   Pp

Mm   Rr   Pp

Pp   Tt   Nn

Bb   Nn   Pp

Pp   Tt   Rr

Ss   Pp   Rr

 Directions: Circle the letters you hear at the beginning of each word.

 Home Activity: Have your child draw pictures of two things that begin with *p*.

© Scott Foresman K

106 Phonics: Consonant *Pp*

Name _____

✎ Draw.

 Directions: If you were Lilly, what would you have written to Mr. Slinger? Write a note or draw a picture.

 Home Activity: Ask your child to tell you why Lilly wrote a note to Mr. Slinger.

Circle.

Rr Ff Pp Ss

 Draw a line.

Pp

 Directions: Circle the letters that begin the word *pen*. Circle the pictures that begin like *pig*. Draw a line under the pictures that begin with *Pp*. Draw a line under the pictures that end like *map*.

108 Phonics: Assessment

© Scott Foresman K

1

Family Times

I Spy Someone

I spy someone who has a bat.
I spy someone who has a cat.
I spy someone who wears a hat.
Let's play "I Spy" together.

I spy someone who has a map.
I spy someone who takes a nap.
I spy someone who wears a cap.
Let's play "I Spy" together.

I spy someone who has a fan.
I spy someone who has a can.
I spy someone who has a van.
Let's play "I Spy" together.

This rhyme features words with the short *a* sound that rhyme with *mat, man,* and *map.*

(fold here)

Name: _____

You are your child's first and best teacher!

Here are ways to help your child practice skills while having fun!

Day 1 Help your child find words in the rhyme on page 1 that have the short *a* sound.

Day 2 Write *big* and *in* on a sheet of paper. Have your child use a finger to trace over the letters, naming each letter aloud. Then have your child use the words *big* and *in* in sentences.

Day 3 Show your child a magazine picture. Ask your child to tell you what is happening in the picture.

Day 4 Ask your child to retell a favorite story.

Day 5 Ask your child to make up and tell a story about a neighborhood party.

Read with your child EVERY DAY!

Phonics Activity: Short a

Maze Directions

Find the way out of the maze.

1. Name all the pictures.
2. Put your pencil on **Start**.
3. Choose the pictures with the short **a** sound.
4. Draw a line to follow the short **a** pictures to the **End**.

Start

End

Name _____

b<u>at</u>    m<u>an</u>    c<u>ap</u>

 Color.

 |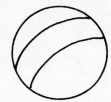

 |

 |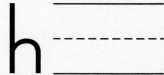

Think Write the endings **ap**, **an**, and **at**.

m _____   f _____   h _____

 Directions: Name the pictures and point to the letters at the end of each word. Color the picture that ends like *cap*, *man*, and *bat*.

 Home Activity: Have your child point to the words at the bottom of the page and say the words aloud.

Name _____

 Write.

_____

- -

_____

_____

- -

_____

 Directions: Tell a story about the pictures. Then write or dictate a telling sentence about one of the pictures.

Home Activity: Have your child tell you a story about something that happened at school today.

112 Grammar: Telling Sentences

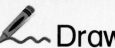 Draw.

Directions: Think of all the places in *Where's the Fly?* Draw a picture that shows the fly in one of these places.

Home Activity: Ask your child to use the picture to tell part of the story.

Name _____

a

✏️ Write.

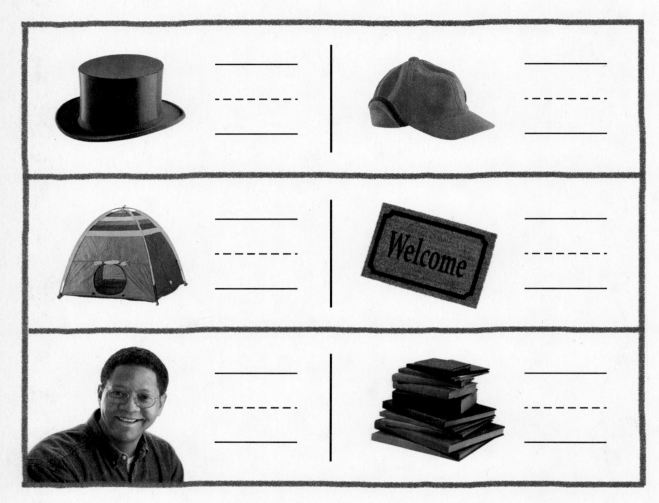

Think Complete the rhyme.

_____

There was a man, _ _ _ _ _ _ _ _ _ _ _ _ _

Who hopped on a _____ .

 Directions: Name the pictures. Then write the letter *a* if the picture has the same middle sound as *fan*.

🎒 **Home Activity:** Ask your child to make up a funny rhyme using words that end with *at*.

Name _____

✏️ Draw.

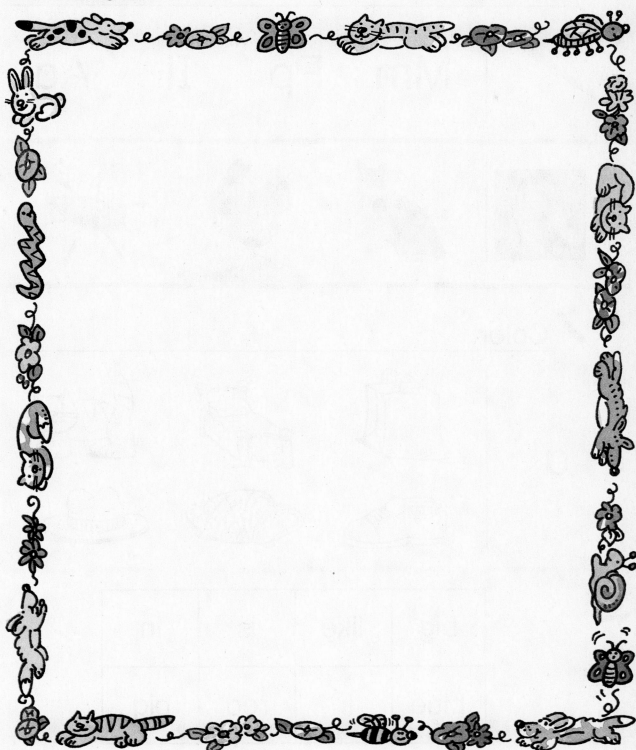

 Directions: Draw a picture of where you would like to land first in the neighborhood if you were the fly in the story.

 Home Activity: Ask your child to name some places a fly would like to visit.

© Scott Foresman K

Draw a line.

 | Mm   Pp   Ii   Aa

  |

 Color.

a |

big	like	is	in
blue	in	red	big

 Directions: Draw a line under the letters that stand for the middle sound in *bat*. Draw a line under the pictures with the same middle sound as in *man*. Color the pictures that have the letter *a* in the middle. Use a yellow crayon to color the words *in* and *big*.

116 Phonics: Assessment

Family Times

If You're Happy

If you're happy and you know it, clap your hands.
If you're happy and you know it, clap your hands.
If you're happy and you know it,
And you really want to show it.
If you're happy and you know it, clap your hands.

. . . hold your head.
. . . hold your heel.
. . . hop right here.
. . . hum this tune.

Read "If You're Happy" with your child. This rhyme features words that begin with *h*.

(fold here)

Name: _____

You are your child's first and best teacher!

Here are ways to help your child practice skills while having fun!

Day 1 Ask your child to name pictures on page 1 that begin with *h*.

Day 2 Help your child find words in the rhyme on page 1 that begin with *h*.

Day 3 Read a story to your child. Then talk about something that happened in the story and why it happened.

Day 4 Your child is learning to make announcements. Play a game together and ask your child to announce the winner.

Day 5 Look at a book together. Ask your child to point to capital letters at the beginning of sentences and periods at the end.

Read with your child EVERY DAY!

Phonics Game: H Words

Game Directions

1. Put a penny on each picture.

2. Choose a picture and say its name.

3. If the picture's name begins with **h**, keep the penny.

4. When you have 6 pennies, say, "happy."

Hh

✏️ **Draw a line.**

✏️ **Write the letters** Hh. _____

_____

 Directions: Draw a line from each hook to a picture that begins with *h*. Draw another hook and another thing that begins with *h*.

 Home Activity: Ask your child to name two animals that begin like *hook,* such as hippopotamus, horse, or hamster.

Maxi, the Hero

 Write. ✎ Draw.

We live here

_____

I go to school

_____

We have a cat

_____

I like to play

_____

 Directions: Circle the capital letters. Write a period at the end of each sentence. Draw a picture for each sentence.

 Home Activity: Ask your child to read each sentence and point to and say each capital letter and each period.

 Draw.

 Directions: Draw a picture to show why the balloon popped.

 Home Activity: Have your child tell you what happened to the balloon and why it happened.

Comprehension: Cause and Effect   **121**

Hh

✏ Write. _____

 **Think** Write the missing letter.

The house sits on a ____ ill.

 Directions: Name each picture. Write *Hh* if the picture begins like *house*.

 Home Activity: Ask your child to name something in your home that begins like *home*.

Name _____

✎ Draw.

Directions: If you were Maxi's owner, how would you reward Maxi for being a hero? Draw a picture of the reward.

Home Activity: Ask your child to tell you how Maxi became a hero.

Reader Response **123**

Name _____

 Circle.

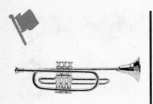

Ss Mm Hh Ff

 Color.

Hh

 Directions: 🚩 Circle the letters that begin the word *horn*. 🦋 Circle the pictures that begin like *horse*. 🔑 Circle the picture that begins like *house*. 🌸 Color the pictures that begin with *Hh*.

1

Family Times

A Girl, a Goat, and a Goose

I am a busy girl, you know.
I have a garden that I grow.
I have a goat and a big grey goose.
One day the goat and goose got loose.
My goat and goose gobbled grapes I grow.
My goat and goose took the garden hoe!
They dug a hole by my garden gate.
When I got there, it was too late.
Now my big dog guards the goat and goose.
My goat and goose will not get loose!

This rhyme features words that begin with g. Say or sing "A Girl, a Goat, and a Goose" with your child to the tune of "Hush, Little Baby."

(fold here)

Name: _____

© Scott Foresman K

You are your child's first and best teacher!

Here are ways to help your child practice skills while having fun!

Day 1 Help your child find the words in the rhyme on page 1 that begin with g.

Day 2 Have your child use the words *shoes, dance, care,* and *walk* in sentences.

Day 3 Read a book together. Help your child compare the story to another familiar story. Ask your child how the stories are alike, and how they are different.

Day 4 Your child practiced making introductions. Have your child introduce you to a favorite stuffed animal.

Day 5 Play a guessing game in which you think of something and your child asks ten questions to try to figure out what you are thinking of.

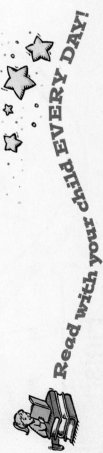

Read with your child EVERY DAY!

Phonics Game: G Words

Game Directions

Play with a partner.

1. Use a coin and 2 markers.

2. Put your markers on **Start**.
   Flip the coin. If it is [penny], move one space.
   If it is [nickel], it is your partner's turn.

3. Each player says the name of the object in the picture where the marker is placed.

4. If the picture name begins with **g**, take another turn. If not, your partner takes a turn.

5. The first player to reach **Finish** is the winner.

Start

Finish

3

Gg

 Circle.

 Write the letters Gg. _____

© Scott Foresman K

Directions: Circle the pictures that begin like *girl*. Say a word that is the opposite of *stop* and begins with the letter *g*.

 Home Activity: Have your child write *Gg* on a card and attach it to something with a name that begins with *g*.

Name _____

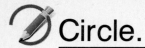 Circle.

What   Who   Where

Who   What   Where

Who   When   Where

Where   What   Who

 Write Who, What, Where, or When.

_____

- - - - - - - - - - - - - - - - -

_____

 Directions: Make up an asking sentence for each picture. Circle the word that starts each. Then write a question word.

 Home Activity: Ask your child to tell you about each picture and make up another question about it.

© Scott Foresman   K

128   *Grammar: Questions*

Name _____

 Make an X.

 Directions: Look at the children's clothes. How are they alike? Different? Put an X on the things that are different.

 Home Activity: Ask your child to make up a story about these two children.

© Scott Foresman K

Comprehension: Compare and Contrast **129**

Name _____

Gg

✏️ Write.

Write a word that begins with **g**.

_____

- -

_____

 Directions: Name the pictures. Write *Gg* next to each picture that begins like *goat*.

 Home Activity: Have your child name things in your home that begin like *girl*.

© Scott Foresman K

130 Phonics: Consonant *Gg*

Name _____

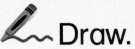 Draw.

 Directions: Draw a new pair of shoes for Miss Alice.

 Home Activity: Ask your child to tell you about the book, *Shoes Like Miss Alice's*.

Circle.

 | **Bb**   **Hh**   **Cc**   **Gg**

 Draw a line.

Gg

 Directions: Circle the letters that stand for the sound at the beginning of the word *goat*. Circle pictures that begin like *goose*. Circle the pictures that end like *dog*. Draw a line under the pictures that begin with *Gg*.

132 Phonics: Assessment

© Scott Foresman K

Family Times

Two Big Pigs

I know two big pigs.
One pig is named Tip.
Tip drives a big rig
And drives his friend Zip.

Tip wears a big hat
And dances the jig.
Zip likes to giggle
And wears a big wig.

Tip eats six big figs.
His clothes never fit.
Zip likes to keep trim
And eats just a bit!

This rhyme features words that have the short *i* sound and the word endings *ig* and *it*. Recite "Two Big Pigs" with your child.

(fold here)

Name: _____

You are your child's first and best teacher!

Here are ways to help your child practice skills while having fun!

Day 1 Help your child find words in the rhyme on page 1 that have the short *i* sound.

Day 2 Have your child use the words *up* and *a* in sentences. Together, look for each word in one of your child's favorite books.

Day 3 Read aloud a favorite story. Then ask your child to tell what happens first, next, and last.

Day 4 Your child is learning to give directions. Have your child give directions for doing a job around your home.

Day 5 Have your child ask you a question. Answer the question. Then ask a question for your child to answer.

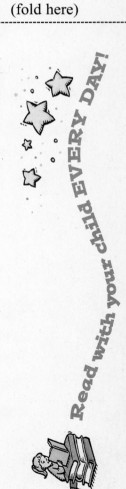

Read with your child EVERY DAY!

Help the Pig

Game Directions

1. Write I i on the pig.
2. Draw a line to show the pig how to get the wig.

i

 Draw a line. _____

(Think) Write the letters I i. _ _ _ _ _ _

 Directions: Draw a line to the pig from pictures with the same middle sound as *sit*. Draw something else in the pen.

 Home Activity: Have your child name words that rhyme with *pit*.

Name _____

 Color.

 Directions: Color the picture that answers *What is the girl painting?* and the one that answers *Who is painting the fence?*

 Home Activity: Ask your child a question about a picture on this page. Then have your child ask you a question.

Name _____

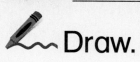 Draw.

 Directions: Draw a picture to show a new beginning for the story *Mrs. McNosh Hangs Up Her Wash.*

 Home Activity: Ask your child to tell a story about how Mrs. McNosh washes her clothes.

Comprehension: Sequence **137**

i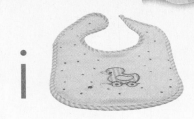

✏️ Write.

 **Think** Write a word that rhymes with **fit**

_____

and begins with **S**. _____

© Scott Foresman K

Name _____

✏️ Draw.

 Directions: Draw something silly
Mrs. McNosh might find at your house
to hang up with the wash.

 Home Activity: Ask your child to tell
about a favorite part of the story
Mrs. McNosh Hangs Up Her Wash.

Name _____

 Circle.

 | Aa Pp Ii Gg

 |

 Draw a line.

i |

a	fit	bat	up
an	up	put	I

Directions: Circle the letters that stand for the sound in the middle of the word *pig*. Name the pictures. Circle the pictures that have the same middle sound as in *fish*. Draw a line under the pictures that have the letter *i* in the middle. Draw a line under the words *up* and *a*.

Family Times

Sat to Sit

Can you hear the **at** in sat and pat?
Can you hear the **it** in sit and pit?
Can you hear when **at** is changed to it?
Like sat to sit or pat to pit?

Can you hear the **ap** in tap and lap?
Can you hear the **ig** in big and pig?
Can you hear when **ap** is changed to ip?
Like tap to tip or lap to lip?

Can you hear the **an** in fan and pan?
Can you hear the **in** in fin and pin?
Can you hear when **an** is changed to in?
Like fan to fin or pan to pin?

This rhyme features words that have the short *a* or short *i* sound.
Read or recite "Sat to Sit" with your child.

(fold here)

Name: _____

You are your child's first and best teacher!

Here are ways to help your child practice skills while having fun!

Day 1 Help your child find words in the rhyme on page 1 that have a short *a* or short *i*. (They are *sat, pat, sit, pit, tap, tip, lap, lip, big, pig, fan, pan, fin,* and *pin*.)

Day 2 Ask your child to think of words that rhyme with *pan* and words that rhyme with *pin*.

Day 3 Read a story to your child. Talk about why things happened in the story and how some events caused others.

Day 4 Your child is learning to follow oral directions. Provide practice for following two-step directions, such as "Put on your socks. Then put on your shoes."

Day 5 With your child, look at advertisements in newspapers or magazines or on display signs. Ask your child to point out question marks.

Read with your child EVERY DAY!

Phonics Game:
Penny Plunk

Game Directions

Play with a friend.
Take turns dropping a penny on the target.

1. If the penny lands on **Pp**, the player says a word that starts with the p sound.

2. If it lands on **Hh**, the player says a word that starts with the h sound.

3. If it lands on **Gg**, the player says a word that starts with the g sound.

4. If it lands on **Ii**, the player says a word with the vowel sound i as in **sit**.

5. If it lands on **Aa**, the player says a word with the vowel sound a as in **sat**.

cat    pig

 Circle.   Draw a line.

Write the letters **a** and **i**.

_____   _____

- - - - - - -   - - - - - - -

_____   _____

 Directions: Circle pictures with the same middle sound as *cat*. Draw a line under pictures with the same middle sound as *pig*.

 Home Activity: Have your child name two things that have the short *a* sound as in *cat* and the short *i* sound as in *wig*.

 Circle.

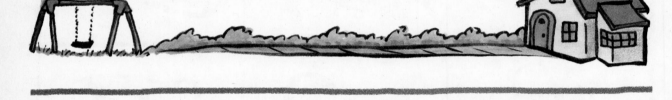

Where do you live?

What game do you like?

Can you see the dog?

Did you go out to play?

 Write.

 Directions: Circle the capital letters and the question marks. Write or dictate your own asking sentence.

Home Activity: Read a story together. Ask your child to listen for questions and look for capital letters and question marks.

© Scott Foresman K

Name 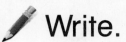 _____

Draw. Write.

 Directions: Look at each picture. Write a word or draw a picture to tell what Ruby would send Max to the store to get.

 Home Activity: Ask your child to make up a story about each of these pictures.

Comprehension: Cause and Effect **145**

Name _____

Hh  Gg Pp

✏️ Write letters.

Think Choose two pictures that begin with the same sound. Use the words in a sentence.

Directions: Say the names of the pictures. Write the capital and lowercase letter that begins the name for each object in the box.

Home Activity: Have your child practice writing the letters *Gg, Hh,* and *Pp* on a separate sheet of paper.

My Little Book

This rhyming book belongs to

_____

Directions Write your name.

✂ (cut here)

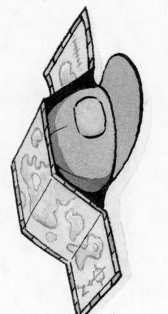

I see a _____ ap on a _____ ap.

(fold here)

I see a _____ ib on a _____ ig.

I see a _____ an with a _____ an.

Directions: Tell what you see. Write the missing letters.

I see a ___ ig in a ___ ig.

Directions: Tell what you see. Write the missing letters.

I see a ___ at on a ___ at.

© Scott Foresman K

I see a ___ at in a ___ at.

I see a ___ an in a ___ an.

Name _____

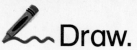 Draw.

 Directions: Look at the block tower that Ruby built. Draw a picture of what may happen when Max walks into the room.

 Home Activity: Ask your child to retell the story *Bunny Cakes* for you.

Circle.

 | Pp   Hh   Gg   Bb

 Color.

Pp |

Hh |

Gg |

 |

Directions: Circle the letters that stand for the sound at the beginning of the word *pig*. Circle the pictures that begin like *hat*. Color the pictures that begin with *Pp*, *Hh*, or *Gg*. Color the picture that rhymes with *cap*.

1

Family Times

A Party for Casey!

It's Casey's party. What can we make?
Cream-filled cookies and a carrot cake!
Count Casey's candles from one to six.
Fill the cups with cocoa mix.
Make a card and color it too.
Color it with crayons, red and blue.
Carry the cake very carefully.
Blow out the candles, one, two, three!

Recite "A Party for Casey!" with your child as a jump rope chant. This rhyme features words that begin with *c* and have the same beginning sound as *Casey*.

(fold here)

Name: _____

You are your child's first and best teacher!

Here are ways to help your child practice skills while having fun!

Day 1 Help your child look for words in the rhyme on page 1 that begin with *C* or *c*.

Day 2 Help your child find the words *get* and *where* in a storybook. Together, read the sentences with these words.

Day 3 Read a story to your child, stopping one or two times to ask what your child thinks will probably happen next.

Day 4 Your child is learning to identify rhyming words in a poem. Read or recite a poem and ask your child, "Which words rhyme? Which words don't rhyme?"

Day 5 Ask your child to use color words to tell what things in your home look like, such as a red book, a blue rug, a white dish.

Read with your child EVERY DAY!

Phonics Game: C Words

Game Directions

1. Use a penny and 2 markers.

2. Flip the penny. If it lands on , move your marker 1 space. If it lands on , move 2 spaces.

3. Name the picture you stop on. If it begins with c, stay there. If it doesn't begin with c, move back 1 space.

4. The first player to reach the end of the river wins.

Start

End

2

3

Cc

Color.

Write the letters Cc.

 Directions: Color the pictures that begin like *car*.

 Home Activity: Ask your child to say the sound at the beginning of *camera* and then say another word that begins with this sound.

Name _____

red

blue

 Color. _____

✏️ Write.

_____   _____

- - - - - - - - - - - - - - - -   - - - - - - - - - - - - - - - -

_____   _____

 Directions: Use a red crayon and a blue crayon. Color each butterfly one color. Then write the color words.

Home Activity: Ask your child to name two red things and two blue things in your home.

Name _____

 Draw.

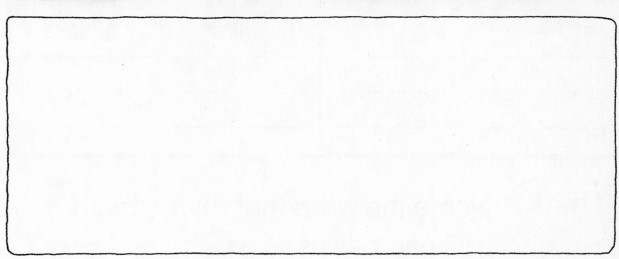

 Directions: Look at the pictures on the page. Draw a picture to show what will probably happen next.

Home Activity: Have your child tell you a story about the pictures on the page, beginning with the top picture.

Comprehension: Predicting **155**

C c

✏️ Write.

(boat) (coat)

(cap) (map of United States)

(car) (star)

(cup) (dog/puppy)

Think Name the word that rhymes with **ball** and begins with **c**.

 Directions: Name the rhyming pictures. Write a capital *C* and lowercase *c* under each picture that begins like *cat*.

 Home Activity: Ask your child to name the pictures on this page that begin with *c*.

Name _____

 Draw.

Directions: Draw a picture to show how you would surprise someone in your family.

 Home Activity: Ask your child to tell you about the surprise in the picture and whom the surprise is for.

Draw a line.

  | **Rr** **Gg** **Tt** **Cc**

  |

 Circle.

Cc |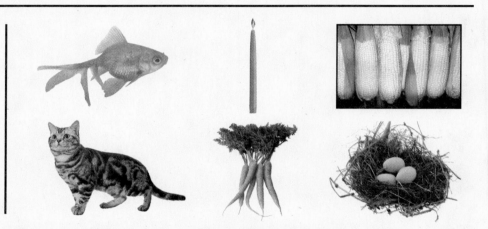

up	cat	where	big	get
I	not	like	where	it

Directions: Draw a line under the letters that stand for the beginning sound in *cup*.  Draw a line under the pictures that begin like *cow*. Circle the pictures that begin with *Cc*. Circle the words *get* and *where*.

Family Times

From a Doggie to a Duck!

See the darling doggie keep the beat.
See the dandy donkey stamp her feet.
See the diving dolphin take a dip.
See the duck do one big flip.

See the darling doggie do a dance.
See the dandy donkey dig and prance.
See the diving dolphin dive so deep.
See the duck go peep, peep, peep!

This rhyme features words that begin with *d*. Recite or sing "From a Doggie to a Duck!" to the tune of "I'm a Little Teapot" with your child.

(fold here)

Name: _____

You are your child's first and best teacher!

Here are ways to help your child practice skills while having fun!

Day 1 Help your child find words in the rhyme on page 1 that begin with *d*.

Day 2 Ask your child to name a word that rhymes with *pot* and begins like *dish*.

Day 3 Have your child choose a favorite story and tell about where it takes place.

Day 4 Your child is learning to listen for details. Read a book with your child once for enjoyment. Before rereading it, ask two or three questions about details. Have your child listen for the answers as you read.

Day 5 Ask your child to use describing words to tell something that happened in school today.

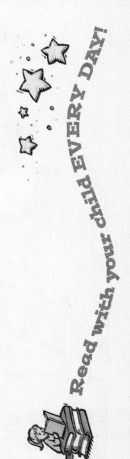

Read with your child EVERY DAY!

Phonics Game: D Words

Game Directions

1. Each player needs a coin and a button. Place the button at **Start**.

2. Take turns flipping the coin.

3. Heads: Move your button to the next picture of a word that begins with **d**.
   Tails: The next player takes a turn.

4. The player whose button reaches **Home** first is the winner.

Start

Home

Name _____

Dd

 Circle.

 Write the letters Dd. _ _ _ _ _ _ _ _ _

 Directions: In each box, circle the picture that begins with *d*. Then write the letters *Dd*.

 Home Activity: Ask your child to name the pictures on this page that begin like *duck*.

Name _____

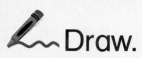 Draw.

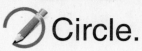 Circle.

big

little

hot

cold

light

heavy

 Directions: Draw something you see outdoors. Circle the words on the right that describe what you drew.

 Home Activity: Have your child say the describing words that match the drawing and use more words to tell about it.

Name _____

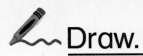 Draw.

What happened?

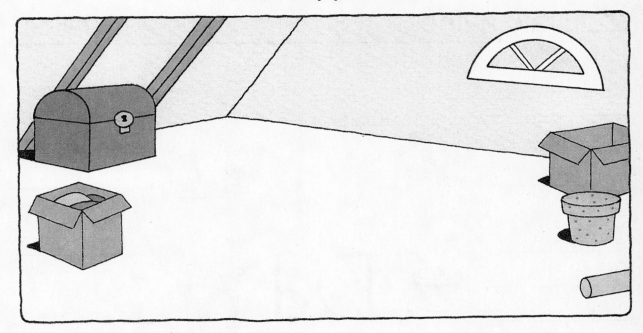

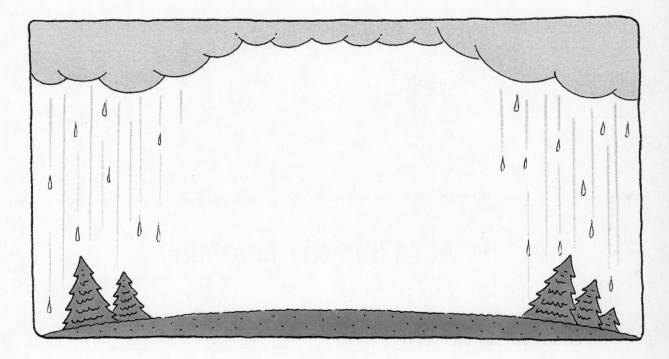

 Directions: What happened in each place in the story? Draw something the characters did there.

 Home Activity: Ask your child to tell you what the characters did in each place.

D d

 Draw a line.

_____   _____
- - - - - - - - - -      - - - - - - - - - -
_____   _____

_____   _____
- - - - - - - - - -   **Dd**   - - - - - - - - - -
_____   _____

_____   _____
- - - - - - - - - -      - - - - - - - - - -
_____   _____

 Write the word that rhymes with **cart**

and begins with **d**.   _____
                          - - - - - - - - - -
                          _____

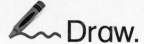 Draw.

 Directions: Draw your favorite part of *In the Rain with Baby Duck.*

 Home Activity: Ask your child to tell what happens in the scene pictured.

Circle.

  | **Bb**   **Cc**   **Dd**   **Ff**

  |

 Dd |

 Draw.

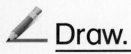 **Directions:** Circle the letters that stand for the beginning sound in *door*.  Circle the pictures that begin like *dog*. Circle the pictures that begin with *Dd*. Draw a picture of something that begins with *d*.

Family Times

Little Ladybugs Laughing

One little ladybug lands on a log.
Two little ladybugs lean on a log.
Three little ladybugs lie on a log.
I see little ladybugs laughing!

Four little ladybugs look at me.
Five little ladybugs leap at me.
Six little ladybugs laugh at me.
I see little ladybugs laughing!

This rhyme features words that begin with *l*. With your child, say or sing "Little Ladybugs Laughing" to the tune of "Skip to My Lou." Then read the rhyme again, a line at a time. Ask your child to find the ladybugs that each line describes.

(fold here)

Name: _____

You are your child's first and best teacher!

Here are ways to help your child practice skills while having fun!

Day 1 Help your child find words in the rhyme on page 1 that begin with *l*.

Day 2 Have your child use the words *one* and *what* in sentences.

Day 3 When you are reading with your child, stop every so often to ask what will happen next, or when you are watching TV together, turn off the set for a moment and ask what will happen next.

Day 4 Have your child show you something made at school and tell you about it.

Day 5 Your child is learning that some words mean "more than one." When you are reading a story, or when you and your child are in a store or other places where you see print, help your child identify words that mean more than one, such as *pears* and *apples*.

Read with your child EVERY DAY!

Phonics Game:
L Words

Game Directions

1. Take turns naming a food on the table. (Review the names of foods with your child.)

2. Put a penny on the picture if its name begins with Ll.

3. When all the pictures beginning with Ll are covered, say three foods with names that begin with Ll that the lion might like. For example, "Lions like lasagne, lemons, and lollipops."

Name _____

¡Fiesta!

L l

🚫 Circle.
_____

 Write the letter for the sound
at the beginning of .

_____
_ _ _ _ _ _ _
_____

Directions: Look at the lobster at the top of the page. *Lobster* begins with *Ll*. Circle each picture that begins with *Ll*.

Home Activity: Have your child write *Ll* on a sticky tag and attach it to something in your home that begins like *lobster*.

 © Scott Foresman K

Phonics: Consonant *Ll* **169**

Write.

cat ____

bug ____

pig ____

frog ____

 Draw.

pans

 Directions: Change each word to make it tell more than one. At the bottom of the page, draw a picture for the word *pans*.

 Home Activity: Have your child tell a story about one of the groups of animals.

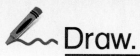 Draw.

 Directions: What could you buy in each store to put in a piñata? Draw a picture of something you could buy at each store.

 Home Activity: Ask your child to make up a story about a shopping trip to one of these stores.

Comprehension: Predicting **171**

Name _____

¡Fiesta!

L l

✏️ Write.

(Think) Make up a sentence using some words that begin like **little**.

 Directions: Say the name of each picture. If it begins like *llama*, write the capital and lowercase *Ll*.

 Home Activity: Have your child draw a picture of a favorite animal or object whose name begins with *l* and write *Ll*.

172 Phonics: Consonant *Ll*

© Scott Foresman K

Name _____

✏️ Draw.

 Directions: You are at the party in *¡Fiesta!* Draw what you would do when the piñata breaks.

 Home Activity: Ask your child to tell you about the picture and some of the things that fell out of the piñata when it broke.

© Scott Foresman K

Reader Response **173**

Name _____

¡Fiesta!

 Circle.

 | **Tt**   **Ll**   **Ff**   **Dd**

  |

 Draw a line.

 Ll |

two	we	one	what	out
what	we	it	out	like

 Directions:  Circle the letters that stand for the beginning sound in *lobster*.  Name the pictures. Circle the pictures that begin like *lion*.  Name the pictures. Draw a line under the pictures that begin with *Ll*.  Draw a line under the words *one* and *what*.

 © Scott Foresman K

174 Phonics: Assessment

Family Times

Once Upon a Time

Once upon a time there was a frog.
Frog had a friend who was a hog.
Hog had a friend who was an ox.
Ox had a friend who was a fox.

Frog liked to hop out of the bog.
Hog liked to plop down in the fog.
Ox liked to sit in a shady spot.
Fox liked to jog and trot a lot.

When it got hot they would hop, hop, hop
Into the pond with a plop, plop, plop!

This rhyme features words that have the short *o* sound, as in *top*, at the beginning or in the middle of the word. Say or sing "Once Upon a Time" with your child to the tune of "Hush, Little Baby."

(fold here)

Name: _____

You are your child's first and best teacher!

Here are ways to help your child practice skills while having fun!

Day 1 Help your child find words in the rhyme on page 1 that rhyme with *not*.

Day 2 Have your child name words that rhyme with *mop*.

Day 3 Read a story together. Help your child compare it to another favorite story. Ask your child to tell how the stories are alike and how they are different.

Day 4 Your child is practicing using descriptions. Ask your child to describe something that happened at school today.

Day 5 Look through a magazine with your child. Ask your child to name people (girl, man), places (airport, garden), and things in the pictures (car, watch).

Read with your child EVERY DAY!

Phonics Activity: Rhyming Words

Activity Directions

1. Name the objects at the left of each path.

2. Name the objects at the right of each path.

3. Trace the path from each object on the left to the object it rhymes with on the right.

 Circle.

 Write the letters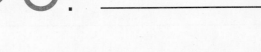

Directions: Circle the pictures that begin like *otter*. Then think of the month that comes after September and begins with *O*.

Home Activity: Have your child think of a name that begins like *otter*.

Draw a line.

 Draw. 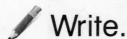 Write.

_____

- - - - - - - - - - - - - - - - - - -

_____

Name _____

 Write.

 Directions: Look at the top picture. Put an X on the things that are different in the bottom picture.

 Home Activity: Ask your child to tell a story about the picture.

Comprehension: Compare and Contrast **179**

Name _____

✏️ Write.

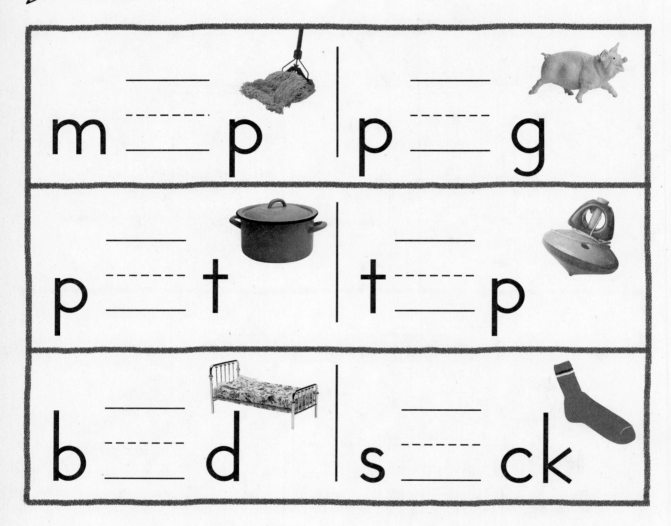

m __ p | p __ g

p __ t | t __ p

b __ d | s __ ck

✏️ Write the word that rhymes with **dot**

and begins with **h**. _____

 Directions: *Dot* has the letter *o* in the middle. Name the pictures. Write *o* for each picture that has *o* in the middle.

 Home Activity: Have your child write the missing vowels in the words that do not have the sound of short *o*.

180 Phonics: Short *o*

Name _____

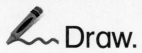 Draw.

 Directions: There are many animals in *Hush! A Thai Lullaby.* Draw a picture of an animal that might wake you.

 Home Activity: Ask your child what sound the animal makes and tell how that sound might disturb a sleeping baby.

Circle.

 | Cc   Tt   Oo   Pp

  |

  |

✏ Draw a line.

Oo

 Directions: 🚩 Circle the capital and lowercase letters that stand for the beginning sound in *otter*. 🦋 Circle the pictures that rhyme with *knot*. 🐛 Circle the pictures that rhyme with *stop*. 🌸 Draw a line under the pictures that begin with *Oo*.

Family Times

Kindergarten Kitty

Kindergarten Kitty kicks the ball.
Kindergarten Kitty is so tall.
Kindergarten Kitty keeps a key.
Kindergarten Kitty is kind to me.

Kindergarten Kitty has a kangaroo.
Kindergarten Kitty plays a kazoo.
Kindergarten Kitty flies a kite.
Kindergarten Kitty gets a kiss goodnight!

"Kindergarten Kitty" features words that begin with *Kk*. Say this rhyme as your child jumps rope.

(fold here)

Name: _____

You are your child's first and best teacher!

Here are ways to help your child practice skills while having fun!

Day 1 Together with your child, say the words in the rhyme on page 1 that begin with *Kk*.

Day 2 Write the words *here* and *three* on a sheet of paper. Ask your child to read the words and then use each word in a sentence.

Day 3 Read a story with your child. Afterward, have your child tell you the most important parts of the story.

Day 4 Your child is learning to ask and answer questions. Read a book together and have your child answer two questions about it. Then encourage your child to ask you two questions about the book.

Day 5 Ask your child to name a person, place, or thing in your home. Then have your child use a word to describe the person, place, or thing.

Read with your child EVERY DAY!

Phonics Activity: K Words

Activity Directions

1. Name the picture in each square.

2. Pick a color and color the square **only** if the name begins with **Kk**.

3. You should color 10 squares.

4. The colored squares spell a word. Say the word.

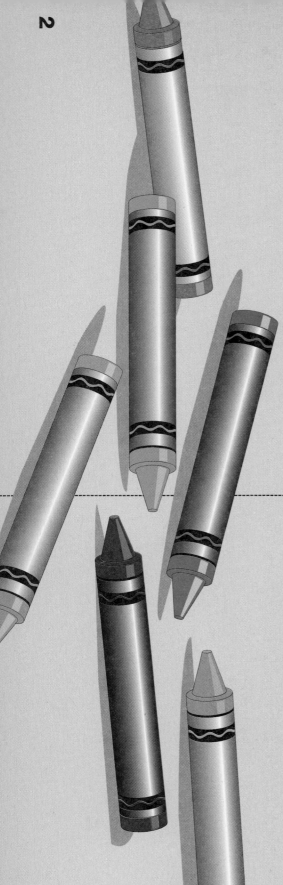

Name _____

K k

✏️ **Color.**

✏️ **Write the letters** **K k** . _____

 Directions: Color the things in the picture that begin with *Kk*. Then write the letters *Kk*.

 Home Activity: Have your child name the things in the picture that begin with *Kk*.

© Scott Foresman K

Phonics: Consonant *Kk* **185**

Name _____

tall    big

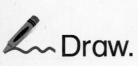 Draw.

Tall	Big

 Directions: Say the describing words. Draw a picture of something that is *tall*. Draw a picture of something that is *big*.

 Home Activity: Ask your child to use describing words to tell about each picture.

© Scott Foresman K

Name _____

 Draw.

 Directions: Draw a picture to show what the story *Three Little Kittens* is about. Tell about your picture.

Home Activity: After reading a favorite story aloud, ask your child to tell you the important parts of the story.

Comprehension: Summarizing **187**

K k

 Write.

_____ What word rhymes with **sit** and

_ _ _ _ _ _ _ _ _ _

begins with **k** ? _____

 Directions: Name each picture. Write *Kk* if the picture begins like *koala*.

 Home Activity: Ask your child to say the word that rhymes with *miss* and begins with *k*.

© Scott Foresman K

Name _____

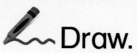Draw.

 Directions: Draw a picture of some part of *Three Little Kittens*. Color the face that shows how you feel about that part.

 Home Activity: Ask your child to tell you which face is colored and why.

Circle.

Ss   Kk   Bb   Ff

 Draw a line.

Kk

one	have	three	like
not	here	what	three

 Directions: Circle the capital and lowercase letters that stand for the beginning sound in *kite*. Circle the pictures that begin like *kangaroo*. Draw a line under the pictures that begin with *Kk*. Draw a line under the words *here* and *three*.

© Scott Foresman   K

Family Times

Can You?

Dive like a duckling.
Cuddle like a cat.
Leap like a lion.
Can you leap like that?

Kick like a kangaroo.
Hum like a hog.
Dig like a donkey.
Can you flop like a frog?

Hop like a hippo.
Clap like a cow.
Trot like a turkey.
Can you show me how?

"Can You?" features words that begin with the letters *c*, *d*, *l*, and *k* and have the short *o* sound as in *hot*. Recite "Can You?" with your child.

(fold here)

Name: _____

You are your child's first and best teacher!

Here are ways to help your child practice skills while having fun!

Day 1 Help your child find words in the rhyme on page 1 that begin with *c*, *d*, *l*, or *k*.

Day 2 Help your child find the words *little* and *two* in a newspaper or magazine.

Day 3 Have your child look at the picture on the cover of a book and predict what the story is about. Then read the book and see if the prediction was correct.

Day 4 Your child is learning to read poems with others in a group. Read a poem to your child. Then have your child recite the poem with you.

Day 5 Ask your child to tell you words that are opposites. Ask: "What is the opposite of *happy*? What is the opposite of *tall*?"

Read with your child EVERY DAY!

Phonics Game: Word Sort

Game Directions

Play with a partner.

1. Find magazine pictures of objects that begin with these letters: **c**, **d**, **l**, and **k**. Place the pictures in a bag.

2. Take turns picking a picture.

3. Say the name of the object and make a check mark under the letter that begins the object's name.

4. When you are finished, count the check marks under each letter.

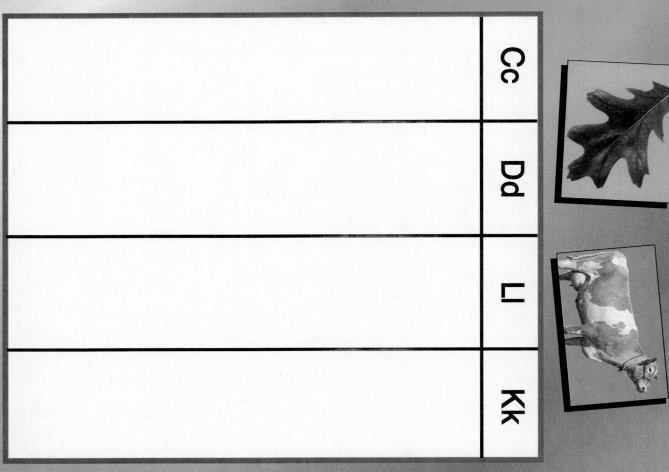

Cc	Dd	Ll	Kk

Name _____

 Draw a line.

Cc Dd

 Ll Kk

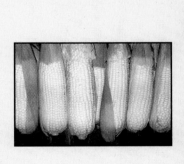

 Directions: Draw a line from each letter at the top to the pictures that begin with that letter.

 Home Activity: Have your child name something in your home that begins with each of the letters at the top of the page.

Five Little Ducks

 Draw a line.

 Directions: Draw a line from the picture in the first column to the picture in the second column that shows the opposite.

 Home Activity: Have your child talk about the opposites on this page.

© Scott Foresman K

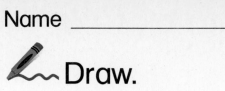

Draw.

 Directions: Draw a picture to show what Mother duck might have done after all the baby ducks came back.

 Home Activity: Have your child tell how the picture shows what Mother duck did when all the baby ducks came back.

Cc Dd Ll

 Write.

Think What word rhymes with **man**

and begins with C ? _____

 Directions: Name each picture. Write the
capital and lowercase letter that begins
each picture.

 Home Activity: Ask your child to circle
the picture of the fruit on this page. Say
the name with your child.

© Scott Foresman K

196 Phonics: Skill Review

My Little Book

This animal book belongs to

___

___

Directions: Write your name.

1

✂ (cut here)

I see three little ___ ats.

___   ___

3

(fold here)

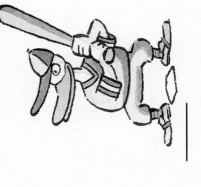

I see a ___ at and a ___ uck.

___   ___

8

I see a ___ uck on a ___ ot.

___   ___

Directions: Tell what you see. Write the missing letters.

6

I see three little ____ ucks.

Directions: Tell what you see. Write the missing letter.

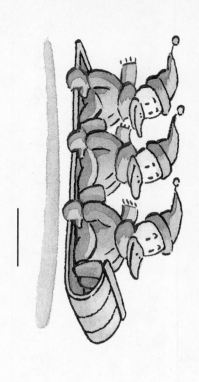

I see a ____ at with a ____ op.

I see three little ____ ambs.

I see three little ____ angaroos.

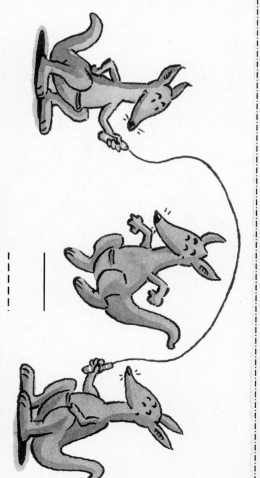

Name _____

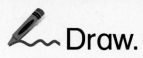Draw.

 Directions: Pretend you are one of the ducks in the story. Draw a picture to show where you would have gone to play.

 Home Activity: Ask your child to talk about a good place for ducks to play.

Circle.

| Cc | Ll | Dd | Dd | Ll | Kk |

| Dd | Kk | Ll | Cc | Ll | Dd |

am	little	hot	like	mop
two	blue	is	two	but

 Write.

_____ _____ _____

- - - - - - - - - - - - - - - - - - - - - - - - - - - - - - - - -

_____ _____ _____

Directions: 🚩 Circle the letters that begin each picture name. 🦋 Circle the words *little* and *two*.
🔑 Write the capital and lowercase letter that begins each picture name.

Family Times

A Journey

Join us on a journey in a jet.
We'll have a jolly time. Ready, get set.

We'll go in January, June, or July.
We'll take a jumbo jet in the sky.

We'll go on a jog to a jungle or two.
We'll take our friend Jan and her puppy too.

We'll see a jackal or jack rabbit jump.
We'll take a jeep that goes bumpety-bump.

This is a jump rope song featuring words that begin with *j*. Recite "A Journey" with your child.

(fold here)

Name: _____

You are your child's first and best teacher!

Here are ways to help your child practice skills while having fun!

Day 1 Take turns with your child finding words in the rhyme on page 1 that begin with *j*.

Day 2 Use the words *we* and *at* in sentences. Then help your child find the words in a storybook.

Day 3 Your child is learning to generalize. Have your child describe the tails of a rabbit, a squirrel, and a pig. Then ask your child to finish this sentence: *Many animals have _____.* (tails)

Day 4 Your child is learning to read orally with expression. Help your child read a familiar book orally with you.

Day 5 Ask your child to use action words to tell about things that are fun to do outdoors.

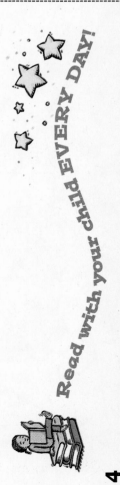

Read with your child EVERY DAY!

Phonics Activity: J Words

Activity Directions

1. Look for things in the picture that begin with Jj.

2. Draw an X on each thing you find.

3. How many different things can you find?

2

3

Jj

✏️ Color.

Jj	Jj

Ss	Kk	Jj	Cc
Pp			Bb
	Ll		Dd
Jj	Jj		Mm

 Think Name a thing that begins with **Jj**.

 Directions: Use a blue crayon to color the spaces with the letters *Jj*. What do you see?

 **Home Activity:** On a calendar, have your child find the months that begin with *J*.

run   jump

 Circle.

_____   _____

- - - - - - - - - - - - - - - -   - - - - - - - - - - - - - - - -

_____   _____

_____   _____

- - - - - - - - - - - - - - - -   - - - - - - - - - - - - - - - -

_____   _____

 Directions: Circle the picture that goes with *run*, and the picture that goes with *jump*. Write each action word where it belongs.

 Home Activity: Ask your child to use *run* and *jump* in sentences.

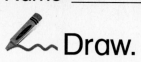 Draw.

 Directions: Draw a picture of what the geese in *Honk! Honk!* will do when it gets warm again. Tell about your picture.

 Home Activity: Have your child tell you what wild geese do when the seasons change.

Jj

🖊 Circle.

✏️ Write the letters Jj. _____

© Scott Foresman K

 Directions: *Jacket* begins with the letter *j*. Circle the things on each shelf that begin like *jacket*.

 Home Activity: Ask your child to name something to drink that begins with *j*.

206 Phonics: Consonant *Jj*

Name _____

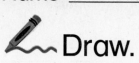 Draw.

 Directions: Pretend you are the child in the story *Honk! Honk!* Draw a picture of one of your adventures.

 Home Activity: Ask your child to tell you about the picture and what is happening in it.

© Scott Foresman K

Draw a line.

 | **Dd** **Hh** **Pp** **Jj**

 Circle.

 Jj |

two	in	we	go	at
it	we	at	up	in

Directions: Draw a line under the letters that begin the word *jar*. ⬥ Draw a line under the pictures that begin like *jug*. ⬥ Circle the pictures that begin with *Jj*. ⬥ Circle the words *we* and *at*.

Family Times

On This Winter Morning

It's time for me to wake up now,
Wake up now, wake up now.
It's time for me to wake up now
On this winter morning.

. . . wash my face.
. . . walk to school.
. . . wave hello.
. . . work today.

This rhyme features words that begin with *w*. Recite "On This Winter Morning" with your child, or sing it to the tune of "The Wheels on the Bus."

(fold here)

Name: _____

© Scott Foresman K

You are your child's first and best teacher!

Here are ways to help your child practice skills while having fun!

Day 1 Help your child find words in the rhyme on page 1 that begin with *w*.

Day 2 Say the words *wolf* and *worm*. Have your child explain why they go together.

Day 3 Show your child a book, a magazine, a newspaper, and a sweater. Ask which two things go together and why.

Day 4 Your child is learning to work with classmates. Help your child decide on a role in family projects.

Day 5 Ask your child to complete these sentences: *A bus driver _____ many passengers.* Remind your child to use *s* at the end of the action word (verb). *The bus _____ a bus.*

Read with your child EVERY DAY!

Phonics Game: W Words

Activity Directions

1. Help Will find his wallet.

2. Find all the paths from Will at the top of the page to his wallet.

3. With a pencil or crayon, trace the path that has only things that begin with the **w** sound.

Name _____

Draw a line.

_____

Write the letters Ww.

- - - - - - - - - - - -

_____

© Scott Foresman K

 Directions: Draw a line from the *Ww* to each thing that begins like *wagon*. Then write the letters *Ww*.

 Home Activity: Ask your child to name one of the two things found in most rooms that begin like *wagon*. (wall, window)

Phonics: Consonant *Ww* **211**

Name _____

 Circle.
_____

Two girls _____ .

skate
skates

One boy _____ .

ride
rides

The boat _____ .

sail
sails

The horses _____ .

run
runs

✏️ Write.

_____

- -

_____

 Directions: Circle the correct action word in each sentence. Write an action word that tells about one person or thing.

Home Activity: Have your child use the action word on the line in a sentence.

Name _____

✎ Draw.

 Directions: Why do the pictures in each box go together? Draw a picture that goes with each set of pictures.

 Home Activity: Ask your child to tell how each set is alike and why each might belong in the book *On the Go*.

Name _____

W w

 Circle.

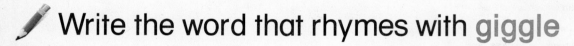 Write the word that rhymes with giggle

----

and begins with W. _____

 Directions: Look for things in the picture that begin like *watch*. Circle each thing that begins with *w*.

 Home Activity: Ask your child to write the letter at the beginning of the word *wiggle*.

Name _____

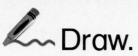 Draw.

 Directions: Invent a new way of travel. Draw your invention.

 Home Activity: Ask your child to describe the picture and the kind of travel it shows.

Name _____

Circle.

Ll Ww Jj Ff

Ww

✏ Write.

_____ _____ _____ _____

- - - - - - - - - - - - - - - - - - - -

_____ _____ _____ _____

Directions: 🚩 Circle the letters that begin the word *wolf*. 🦋 Circle the pictures that begin like *window*. 🔑 Circle the pictures that begin with *Ww*. 🌷 Write the letter *w* on the line under each picture that begins like *wolf*.

Family Times

Vacation

Vacation, vacation is here today.
Let's rent a video and then we'll play.
Let's play volleyball all day long.
Let's play violin and sing a song.

Let's take a trip in a very big van.
Let's buy some veggies from the vegetable man.
Let's each wear a velvet vest.
Vacation, vacation is the best!

This rhyme features words that begin with the *v* sound. Recite "Vacation" with your child to the tune of "Pat-a-Cake." Repeat the rhyme, this time making a V for victory sign with your fingers each time you say a word that begins with *V*.

(fold here)

Name: _____

You are your child's first and best teacher!

Here are ways to help your child practice skills while having fun!

Day 1 Help your child find words in the rhyme on page 1 that begin with *v*.

Day 2 Ask your child to write two words that begin with *v*.

Day 3 After reading a story together, ask your child to tell you what the story was all about.

Day 4 After watching a TV show together, ask your child to tell you what the show was all about.

Day 5 Your child is learning to use complete sentences. Ask your child to use complete sentences to tell you about a favorite game.

Read with your child EVERY DAY!

Phonics Game: V Words

Activity Directions

1. Look at the fruits and vegetables in the picture.

2. Help Mr. Jones load his van.

3. Circle only the pictures of vegetables.

4. How many different vegetables did you find?

Vv

 Circle.

 Write the letters Vv. _____

 Directions: Circle the picture if it begins like *vest*. Then write the letters *Vv*.

 Home Activity: Help your child find the letter *v* on the brand names of products and appliances in your home.

Name _____

   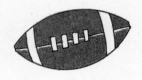

 Draw.

Han plays [ ] .

Tony plays [ ] .

Mary plays [ ] .

Leroy plays [ ] .

 Directions: Draw a ball in each box to complete the sentences. Then say each sentence aloud.

 Home Activity: Ask your child to make up a story about one of the children on this page.

220 Grammar: Complete Sentences

Name _____

 Write.

baseball	first	strike	bat
park	blue	second	catch
base	yellow	home run	throw

_____

- -

_____

_____

- -

_____

_____

- -

_____

 Directions: Look at the picture. Read the words with me. What is the picture about? Write a sentence about the picture.

 Home Activity: Ask your child to make up a story about the picture.

Comprehension: Main Idea **221**

Vv

✏️ Write.

💭 **Think** Make up a sentence using three words that begin like **very**.

 **Directions:** Say the picture names. Write the capital and lowercase *V* next to a picture if it begins like *van*.

 Home Activity: Help your child find *Vv* in signs in your neighborhood.

Name _____

✏️ Draw.

 Directions: Draw a picture to show another way Franklin, Goose, Beaver, and Rabbit could use teamwork to get something done.

 Home Activity: Ask your child to talk about the picture and tell you how the characters are using teamwork.

Circle.

  | **Bb   Ww   Ff   Vv**

  Draw a line.

Vv

 Directions: Circle the letters that stand for the beginning sound in *vest*. Circle the pictures that begin like *vine*. Draw a line under the pictures that begin with *Vv*.

Family Times

Big Enough for Ten!

Let's build a little pen
For the chicks and mother hen.
Let's build a little nest for them
That's big enough for ten!

Let's put the little nest
Where everyone can rest.
Let's build a tent where we can play.
We really did our best!

This rhyme features words that have the short *e* sound and the word endings *en* and *et*. Recite "Big Enough for Ten!" with your child.

(fold here)

Name: _____

You are your child's first and best teacher!

Here are ways to help your child practice skills while having fun!

Day 1 Help your child find words in the rhyme on page 1 that have the short *e* sound as in *bed*.

Day 2 Have your child use the words *that* and *you* in sentences. Together, look for the words in one of your child's favorite books.

Day 3 Give your child six objects, such as a sock, a shoe, a glove, a pen, a pencil, and a crayon. Ask your child to put the objects into groups that belong together.

Day 4 Your child is reading about machines. Talk with your child about a machine in your home.

Day 5 Your child is learning to use complete sentences. Name a member of your family and have your child make up a sentence about something that person can do.

Read with your child EVERY DAY!

Phonics Activity: What Is It?

Activity Directions

1. Look at the puzzle.
2. Name the letters you see.
3. Color the pieces with E or e.
4. What do you see?

E   e

e   E

y   P   H   z   L

E

e

e

E

e

j   R

e

e

E

E

E

m   Q   c   T   v

E

i

s

E e 🥚

✏️ Circle.

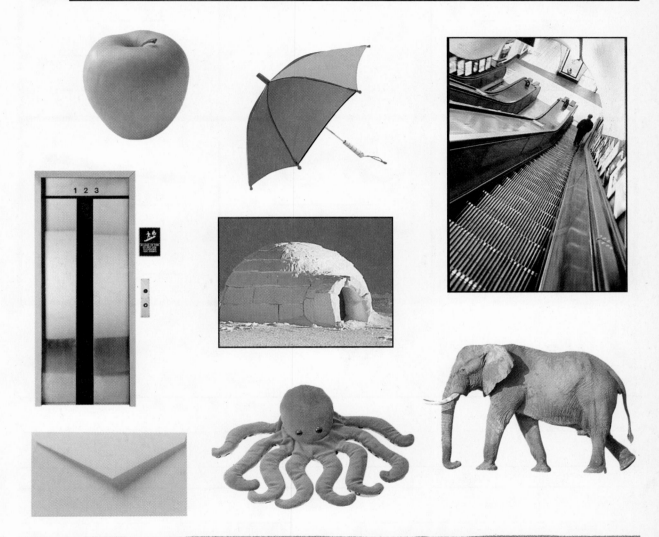

━━━━━━━━━━━━━━━━━━━━━━━━━

🖊️ Write the letters E e. _____ _____

 Directions: Name each picture. Circle the picture if it begins like *egg*.

 Home Activity: Help your child name other words that begin with the short *e* sound.

Write.  Circle.

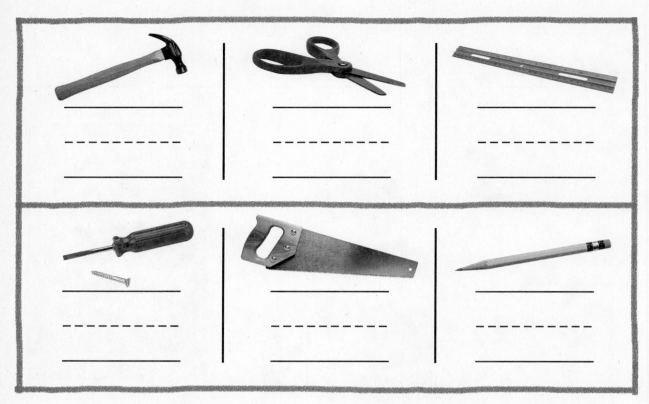

 Write.

_____

_____

_____

_____

 Directions: Write the letter at the beginning of each tool's name. Circle one of the tools. Write a sentence to tell about that tool.

 Home Activity: Have your child make up a sentence about a tool on this page.

Draw a line.

Work

Play

 Directions: Draw a line from the word *Work* to each picture of someone working; from the word *Play* to someone playing.

 Home Activity: Ask your child to name one more activity that goes with *Work* and one more that goes with *Play*.

e

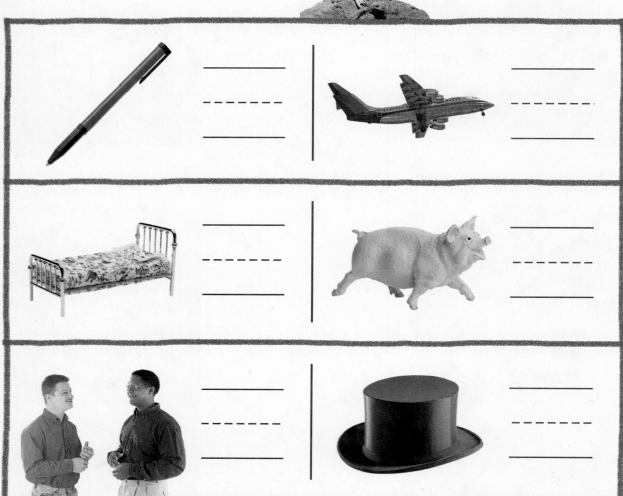

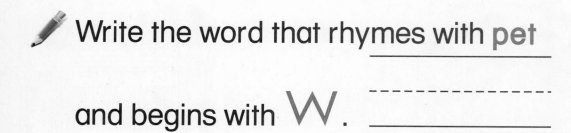
Write the word that rhymes with pet _____

and begins with W. _____

Name _____

✏️ Draw.

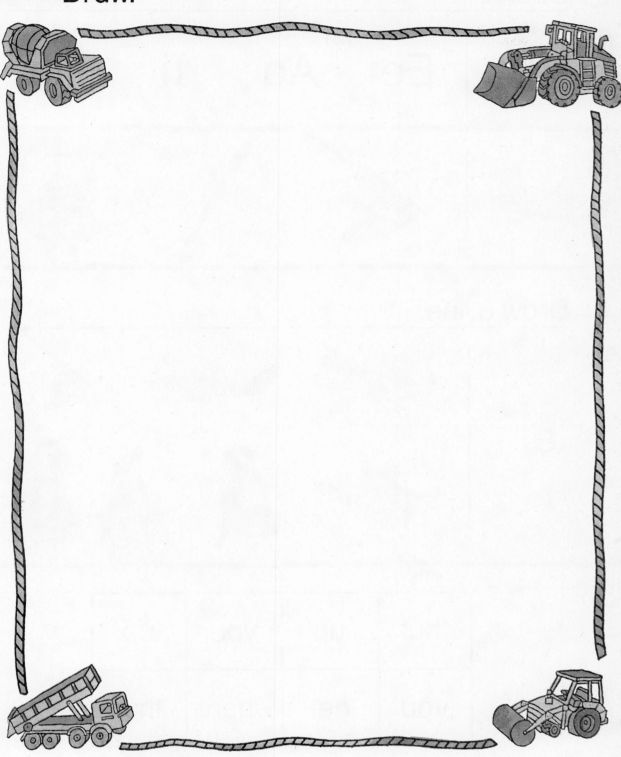

Directions: Think about the machines in the story. Draw a picture of something you would build with a machine.

Home Activity: Ask your child to tell what the machine in the picture is doing.

Circle.

  | # Ee Aa Ii Hh

 ## Draw a line.

e |

that	up	you	up
you	get	where	that

Directions: Circle the letters for the sound in the middle of the word *hen*. Name the pictures. Circle the pictures that have the short *e* sound as in *bed*. Draw a line under the pictures that have the letter *e* in the middle. Draw a line under the words *that* and *you*.

Family Times

A Quilt

Queen will make a quilt today.
She'll work quickly all the day.

In the squares she'll stitch a Q
And a little quail that's blue.

She'll work quietly on this day.
Then she'll quit and go to play.

This rhyme features words that begin with *q*. Sing "A Quilt" with your child to the tune of "Twinkle, Twinkle, Little Star."

(fold here)

Name: _____

You are your child's first and best teacher!

Here are ways to help your child practice skills while having fun!

Day 1 Have your child point to the pictures on page 1 that begin with *q*.

Day 2 As you read the rhyme on page 1, help your child find words that begin with *q*.

Day 3 Remind your child of the rhyme "A Quilt." Ask your child to tell in one sentence what this rhyme is mostly about.

Day 4 Your child is learning to listen to new words. Read or recite an unfamiliar rhyme. Ask your child to name a new word. Talk about what the word means.

Day 5 Ask your child to tell you about something that happened yesterday. Encourage your child to use words that tell what happened in the past.

Read with your child EVERY DAY!

Phonics Activity: Q Words

Activity Directions

1. Use two different color crayons.

2. Color the squares Q with one color.

3. Color the squares q with the other color.

4. Talk about your quilt.

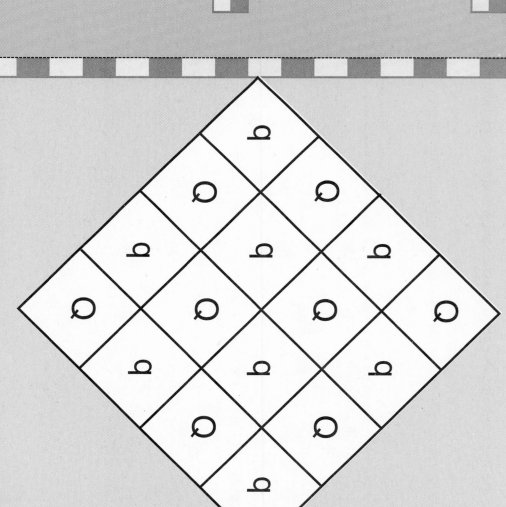

Q q ❓

 Draw a line.

 Write the letters Q q. _____

 Directions: Name the pictures on the page. Draw a line from each picture that begins with *Qq* to a question mark.

 Home Activity: Ask your child to name the *Qq* things on this page.

Name _____

 Circle.

1. Dad uses a shovel.

2. He dug a big hole.

3. Dad pulls the tree.

4. We planted the tree.

✏️ Write.

_____

- -

_____

 Directions: Listen to each sentence and
circle those about the past. Write one of
the action words about the past.

 Home Activity: Ask your child to use
the action word written at the bottom of
the page in a new sentence.

Name _____

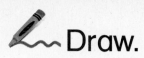 Draw.

 Directions: Draw a picture that shows an important part of *Mike Mulligan and His Steam Shovel*.

 Home Activity: Ask your child to tell you about the picture in one sentence.

Comprehension: Summarizing **237**

© Scott Foresman   K

 Write.

 ------------ ‾‾‾‾‾‾‾  ------------ ‾‾‾‾‾‾‾

 ------------ ‾‾‾‾‾‾‾  ------------ ‾‾‾‾‾‾‾

 ------------ ‾‾‾‾‾‾‾ ------------ ‾‾‾‾‾‾‾

 Write the word that rhymes with **pick**

‾‾‾‾‾‾‾‾‾‾‾‾

----

and begins with q. ‾‾‾‾‾‾‾‾‾‾‾‾

 Directions: A *quail* is a bird. *Quail* starts with *Qq*. Write the letters *Qq* if the picture begins like *quail*.

Home Activity: Have your child name another word that begins with *Qq*.

© Scott Foresman K

238 Phonics: *Qq*

Name _____

 Draw.

 Directions: Draw a picture that shows a different ending for the story *Mike Mulligan and His Steam Shovel*.

 Home Activity: Ask your child to tell you about the new ending for the story.

Circle.

Ll Qq Vv Bb

 Draw a line.

Qq

 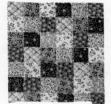 

 Directions: Circle the letters that begin the word *queen*. Circle the pictures that begin like *quail*. Draw a line under the pictures that begin with *Qq*.

1

Family Times

Let's Take a Trip

Vacation's here . . . .
Let's go out west . . . .
Jen packs the bags . . . .
Ben does the rest . . . .

They take a van . . . .
Not a big jet . . . .
They bring a cat . . . .
His name is Chet . . . .

Jen brings a quilt . . . .
Ben wears a vest . . . .
Vacation is . . . .
The very best . . . .

This rhyme features short vowel words and words that begin with *v, w, j,* and *q*. Recite "Let's Take a Trip" with your child.

(fold here)

Name: _____

You are your child's first and best teacher!

Here are ways to help your child practice skills while having fun!

Day 1 Help your child find words in the rhyme on page 1 that have the short *e* sound and the short *i* sound.

Day 2 Have your child name words that begin with each of these letters: *q, j, v,* and *w.*

Day 3 Ask your child to name three things that are used for eating.

Day 4 Have your child tell you about the story *A House Is a House for Me.*

Day 5 Help your child write a telling sentence and an asking sentence (question) about something that happened in school.

Read with your child EVERY DAY!

Ted's House to Ned's House

Activity Directions

Help Ted get to Ned's house.

1. Color the letters J or j yellow.

2. Color the letters V or v blue.

3. Color the letters W or w green.

4. Color the letters Q or q brown.

Follow the path you colored from Ted's house to Ned's house.

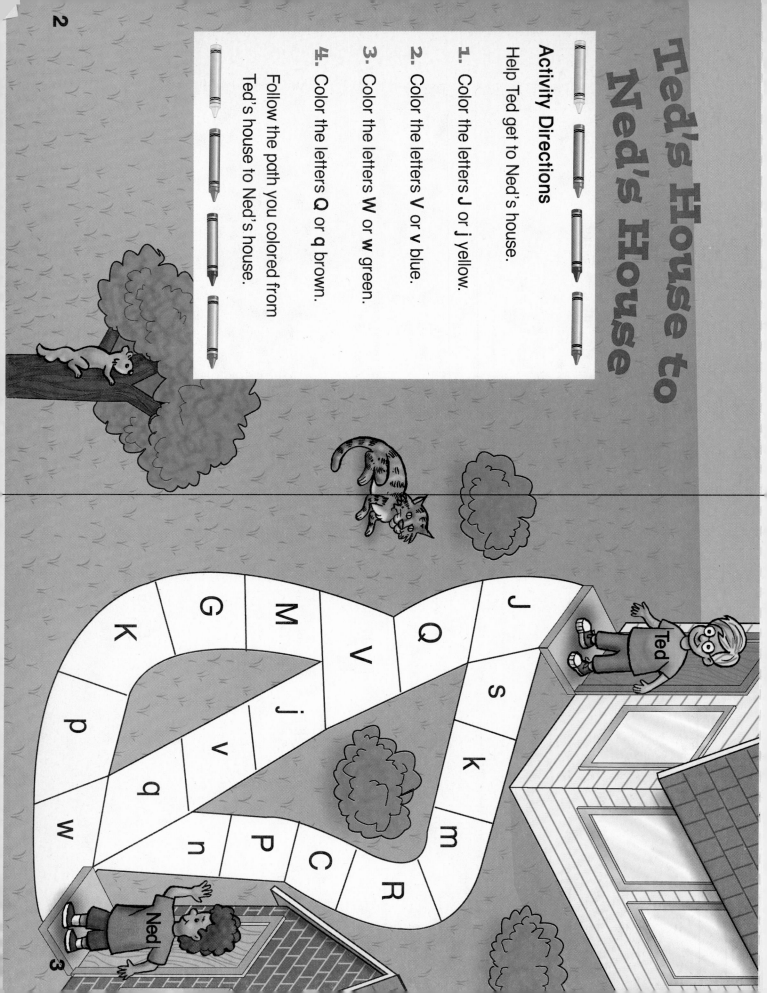

Draw a line.

Jj Vv Ww Qq

Think Circle the pictures that could be houses for things.

 Directions: Draw a line from each letter at the top to the pictures that begin with that letter.

 Home Activity: Have your child practice writing the capital and lowercase *Jj, Vv, Ww,* and *Qq.*

Name _____

 Draw a line.

What is a house for a ?

What is a house for an  ?

What is a house for a  ?

What is a house for a  ?

 Write.

_____

- -

_____

- -

_____

 Directions: Listen to each asking sentence. Draw a line to the picture that answers it. Write a telling sentence about one picture.

Home Activity: Have your child make up an asking sentence using the model on this page.

244 Grammar: Types of Sentences

Name _____

✏️ **Circle.**

 Directions: Look at the pictures in each box. How are they alike? How are they different? Circle those that go together.

 Home Activity: Ask your child to tell you why the things that are circled in each box go together.

Name _____

Jj Vv Ww Qq

🖊 Write.

🖊 Write the word that rhymes with **nest**

_____

- - - - - - - - - - - - - - - - -

and begins with V. _____

 Directions: Name each picture. Write the capital and lowercase letters that begin each picture.

 Home Activity: Ask your child to group the pictures by the beginning letters and tell you the groups and the letter names.

246 Phonics: Skill Review

I can see a ___ ueen.

Now it is time to *quit*!

8

My Little Book

This little book belongs to

_____

_____

_____

_____

_____

Directions: Write your first and last name.

✂ (cut here)

(fold here)

1

I can see.

6

I can ___ alk.

3

____
- - - - -
I can ____ og.

Directions: Tell what you see.
Add the missing letters.

2

____ ____
- - - - - - - - - -
t ____ ____ red hens.

7

We can play

____
- - - - -
____ olleyball.

4

5

© Scott Foresman K

Name _____

 Draw.

 Directions: Think of something not shown in the story that has a house. Draw a picture of it and its home.

 Home Activity: Ask your child to use this sentence to tell about the picture: *A ___ is a house for a ___ .* (place, object, or animal)

Circle.

Jj   Qq   Vv   Jj   Qq   Vv

Jj   Qq   Ww   Jj   Qq   Ww

 Draw a line.

we	like	the	you	who
one	I	that	but	at

Directions: Circle the letters that begin each picture name. Draw a line under the words *we, at, that,* and *you.*

Family Times

The Yak and Zebra

The yak is in the zoo.
He yells to me and you.
He sings a Yankee Doodle doo
And yodels a yahoo!

The zebra is alone,
In the Zebra Zone.

He zig zags and he zips around
And then plays xylophone.

The zebra's name is Zak.
Yanni is the yak.
They eat some zesty ziti now
For a yummy snack.

This rhyme features words that begin with *x*, *y*, and *z*. Say or sing "The Yak and Zebra" with your child to the tune of "The Farmer in the Dell."

(fold here)

Name: _____

You are your child's first and best teacher!

Here are ways to help your child practice skills while having fun!

Day 1 Help your child find words in the rhyme on page 1 that begin with *x*, *y*, or *z*.

Day 2 Have your child write the words *yellow* and *my* and then use the words in sentences.

Day 3 Read the title and author of a book to your child. Ask your child what the story will be like. Will it be funny, sad, or exciting? Why?

Day 4 Your child is practicing speaking well. Encourage your child to speak in complete sentences.

Day 5 Your child is learning about words that name things. Play a naming game. Pick a category, such as things that fly, things with wheels, things we eat for lunch, and so on. See how many things each of you can name for the category.

Read with your child EVERY DAY!

What Animal Is It?

Activity Directions

1. Look at the puzzle.

2. Name the letters you see.

3. Choose two different crayons. Use one crayon to color the pieces with **Z** or **z**.

4. Use the other crayon to color the pieces with **Y** or **y**.

5. Write the letter to complete the name of each animal.

A   F   S

___ ___ a k

___ ___ e b r a

Name _____

Xx  Yy  Zz

 Circle.

 Directions: Name each picture. Circle the pictures with an *x* in green, those with a *z* in blue, and those that begin with *y* in red.

 Home Activity: Help your child name other words that end with *x* or begin with *y* or *z*.

© Scott Foresman K

Phonics: Consonants *Xx*, *Yy*, and *Zz* **253**

Draw a line.

Things at Home	Things at School

 Directions: Read the words in the box. Look at the pictures. Draw a line from each picture to the box where it belongs.

 Home Activity: Have your child name the objects in each group.

Circle and Draw.

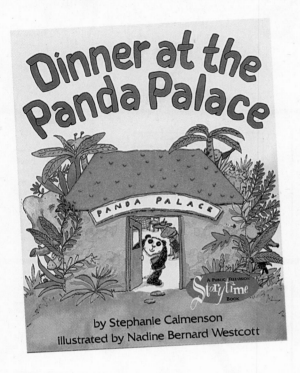

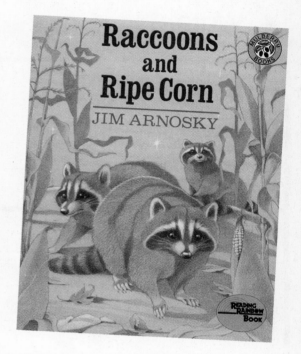

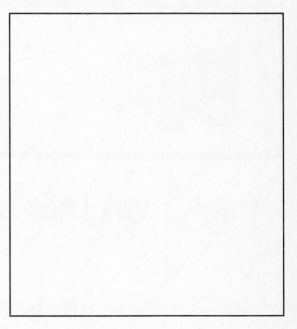

 Directions: Circle the fun story in red. Circle the story that teaches in blue. Draw a cover for another story. Circle it.

 Home Activity: Choose a favorite book of your child's. Talk with your child about why the author wrote the book.

Name _____

Xx  Yy⊙ Zz

✏️ **Write.**

💭 **Think**   What has 12 months

_____

- - - - - - - - - - - - - - - - - -

and starts with **Y** ?   _____

🍎 **Directions:** Say the name of each picture.
If it begins with *y* or *z*, write *y* or *z*. If it
ends with *x*, write *x*.

🎒 **Home Activity:** Help your child look for
words that begin with *y* or *z* in a book.

256   Phonics: Consonants *Xx, Yy, Zz*

Name _____

 Draw.

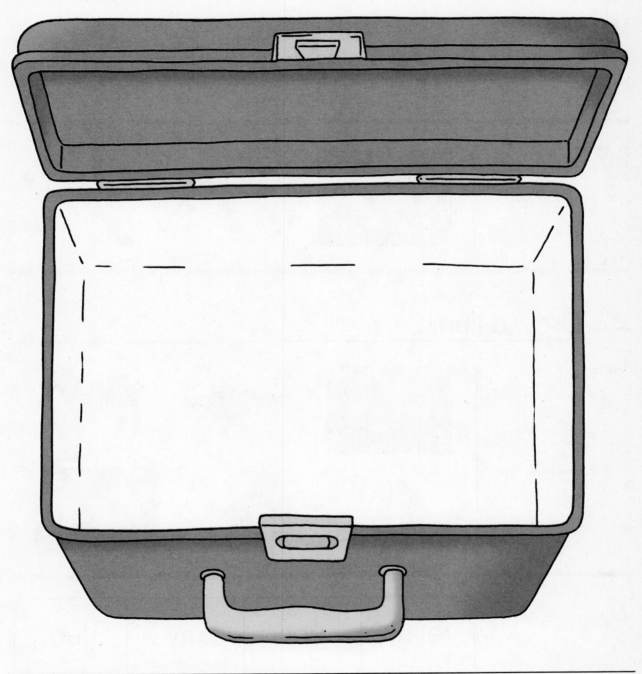

_____

- -

_____

 Directions: If you had a brand-new lunch box, what would you keep in it? Draw a picture and write the name.

 Home Activity: Ask your child to tell why the boy in the story wanted a lunch box.

Reader Response **257**

Name _____

 **Circle.**

 | **Yy   Ww   Zz   Ss**

 Draw a line.

Zz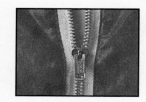

yellow	yes	my	yum
my	yellow	yells	me

 Directions: Circle the letters that begin the word *yo-yo*. Name the pictures. Circle the pictures that end like *box*. Draw a line under the pictures that begin with *Zz*. Draw a line under the words *yellow* and *my*.

Family Times

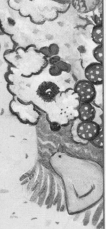

My Puppy

I have a fuzzy puppy.
My puppy likes his rug.
My puppy likes to snuggle
And likes to get a hug.

My puppy likes to chase bugs.
My puppy likes to run.
My puppy likes to jump and tug
And have a lot of fun!

My puppy likes to eat nuts.
My puppy likes to hum.
My puppy likes his little duck
And likes to play the drum.

The rhyme "My Puppy" features words with short *u*. Sing or recite the rhyme with your child.

(fold here)

Name: _____

You are your child's first and best teacher!

Here are ways to help your child practice skills while having fun!

Day 1 Take turns with your child naming words in the rhyme on page 1 that have a short *u*.

Day 2 Ask your child to name words that rhyme with *nut*.

Day 3 Read a story to your child. Then ask your child to tell you about one of the characters.

Day 4 Your child is learning to use proper grammar. Read sentences from a story and talk about the action words (verbs) with your child. For example, "Corduroy *climbed* down the stairs."

Day 5 Have your child use describing words (adjectives) to tell you about things in your home.

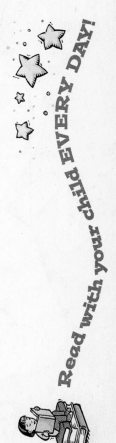

Read with your child EVERY DAY!

Phonics Activity: Short u Words

Activity Directions

1. Use brown and orange crayons.

2. Say the word for each picture.

3. Color the space orange if the word has a short u.

4. Color it brown if the word does not have short u.

U u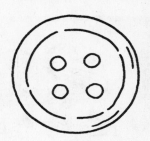

 Color.

 | 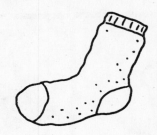 |

 |  |

 |  |

 Write the letters U u.

Directions: Color the pictures that have a short *u* sound. Name something you do with scissors that has a short *u* sound.

Home Activity: Ask your child to name two things in your home that have the short *u* sound as in *hug*.

Name _____

wet  old

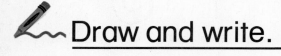 Write.

_____

- - - - - - - - - - -

_____

_____

- - - - - - - - - - -

_____

✎ Draw and write. _____

_____

- -

_____

 Directions: Write the word that describes each picture. Draw a picture of another describing word and write the word.

 Home Activity: Help your child think of other words that describe the pictures.

© Scott Foresman K

Draw and write.

- -

 Directions: Write a word that tells how Corduroy felt when he knocked over the lamp. Draw a picture of what he did next.

Home Activity: Ask your child to tell you about the bear in the picture.

Comprehension: Drawing Conclusions **263**

u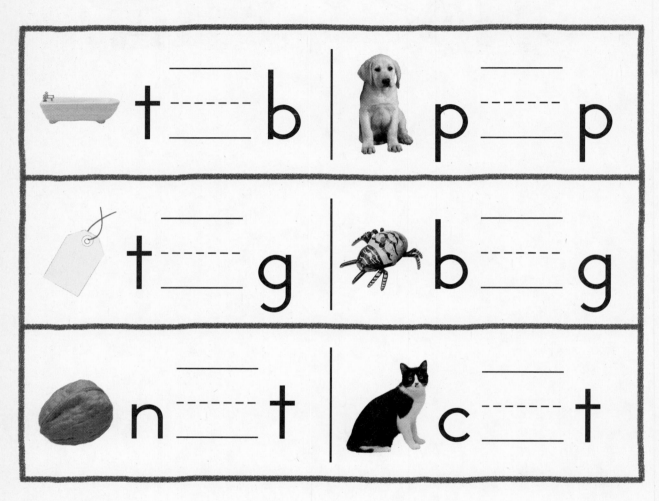

✏️ Write.

t _ _ _ _ _ b		p _ _ _ _ _ p	
t _ _ _ _ _ g		b _ _ _ _ _ g	
n _ _ _ _ _ t		c _ _ _ _ _ t	

💭 **Think** Which picture rhymes with cup?

_____

- - - - - - - - - - - - - - - - -

_____

 Directions: Name each picture. If the picture has the short *u* sound like in *sun*, write the letter *u* in the word.

 Home Activity: Ask your child to say words that rhyme with *bun*.

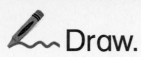Draw.

 Directions: Pretend you are Corduroy. Draw a picture to show where else you could look for a button.

 Home Activity: Ask your child to explain this part of the story.

Draw a line.

Ee Aa Oo Uu

 Circle.

Uu

 Directions: Draw a line under the letters that begin the word *umbrella*. Draw a line under the pictures that have short *u* like in *pup*. Circle the pictures that have the letter *u* in the middle.

Family Times

My Rocket on the Moon

I see a pig on a mat.
I see a hen with a hat.
I see a pup and a cat.
I'm in my rocket on the moon.

I see the pig give a hug.
I see the pup playing tug.
I see them all catch a bug.
I'm in my rocket on the moon.

I see the pig with a mop.
I see the hen go hop, hop.
I see the pup go plop, plop!
I'm in my rocket on the moon.

This rhyme features words with short vowel sounds. Recite "My Rocket on the Moon" with your child.

(fold here)

Name: _____

You are your child's first and best teacher!

Here are ways to help your child practice skills while having fun!

Day 1 Help your child find words in the rhyme on page 1 that have the same short vowel sounds as *pig, mat, hen, pup,* and *mop.*

Day 2 Write the words *see* and *and* on paper and take turns using each word in a sentence.

Day 3 Read a story to your child. Then have your child tell you what happened first, next, and last.

Day 4 Your child is learning to give an oral report. Ask your child to tell you about the moon.

Day 5 Ask your child to use action words, such as, *run, throw, jump* to tell what is fun to do outside.

Read with your child EVERY DAY!

Phonics Game: Short Vowel Words

Game Directions

Help the spaceship reach the moon.
You need 10 markers.

1. Name the first picture near the nose of the rocket. Put a marker on it.

2. Find the letter that stands for the short vowel sound in its name. Color that part of the spaceship.

3. Name the next picture and color that letter on the spaceship.

4. When you have covered all the pictures and colored all the letters, the spaceship can LIFT OFF!

c<u>a</u>t   h<u>e</u>n   m<u>i</u>tt   m<u>o</u>p   b<u>u</u>g

 Draw a line.

a   e   i   o   u

 Write the letter that stands for the ____

middle sound in **fun**. ------

Directions: Name each picture. Draw a line from each picture to the letter that stands for its short vowel sound.

Home Activity: Have your child name things in your home that have short vowel sounds.

sits   hits   hops   hugs

✏️ Write.

 Directions: Read each action word. Write each word under the picture that shows the action.

 Home Activity: Ask your child to use each action word in a sentence.

Name _____

Zoom! Zoom! Zoom!
I'm Off to the Moon!

first   next   last

 Write.

_____

- - - - - - - - - - - -

_____

_____

- - - - - - - - - - - -

_____

_____

- - - - - - - - - - - -

_____

 Directions: Decide which picture comes first, next, and last. Write the words that show the correct order.

 Home Activity: Have your child tell you a story about the pictures, using the words *first*, *next*, and *last*.

Comprehension: Sequence **271**

a   e   i   o   u

 Write.

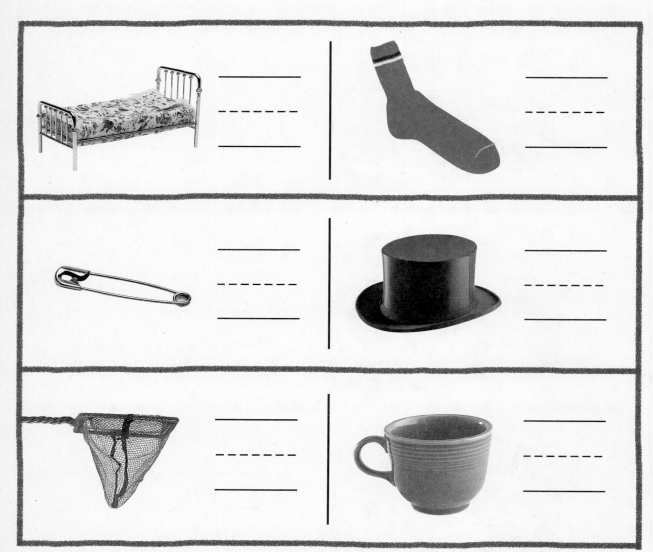

 **Think** Name three words that end with **at**.

Directions: Name each picture. Write the letter that stands for the short vowel sound you hear in each word.

 Home Activity: Ask your child to say the short *e* words on this page.

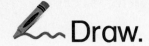 Draw.

 Directions: Draw a picture of yourself in one part of *Zoom! Zoom! Zoom! I'm Off to the Moon!* Show how you feel.

 Home Activity: Ask your child to tell you what happened in this part of the story.

© Scott Foresman K

 Circle.

  | e   a   o   i

  |

 Draw a line.

a |

i |

as	see	red	not	see
hug	can	and	up	three

 Directions: Circle the letter that stands for the middle sound heard in *sock*. Circle the pictures that have the same vowel sound as in *nut*. Name the pictures. Draw a line under the pictures that have an *a* or *i* in the middle. Draw a line under the words *see* and *and*.

274 Phonics: Assessment

Family Times

I Spy Words

I spy words to change around.
I add an **e** and change their sounds.

I spy a tub and an inner tube.
I spy a cub and a cold ice cube.

I spy a can and a candy cane.
I spy a pan and a window pane.

I spy a tap dancer and some tape.
I spy a cap and a big red cape.

This rhyme features words that have short vowels and words that have long vowels, such as *cap* and *cape*. Recite "I Spy Words" with your child.

(fold here)

Name: _____

You are your child's first and best teacher!

Here are ways to help your child practice skills while having fun!

Day 1 Help your child find words in the rhyme on page 1 that have the long *a* sound.

Day 2 Have your child use the words *look* and *to* in sentences. Together, look for each word in one of your child's favorite books.

Day 3 Tell your child a riddle such as "I purr and my name rhymes with *sat*." Have your child guess the answer and tell what clues led to the answer.

Day 4 Your child is learning how to speak to different audiences. Ask your child to pretend that you are a friend who wants to know where to put something away.

Day 5 Have your child name some action words and use them in sentences.

Read with your child EVERY DAY!

Mary Mouse

Activity Directions

Help Mary Mouse get to her home.

1. You need a coin and buttons or markers.

2. Toss a coin. If it lands on heads, move 1 space. If it lands on tails, move 2 spaces.

3. Name each picture as you go. Tell if it has a long vowel sound or a short vowel sound.

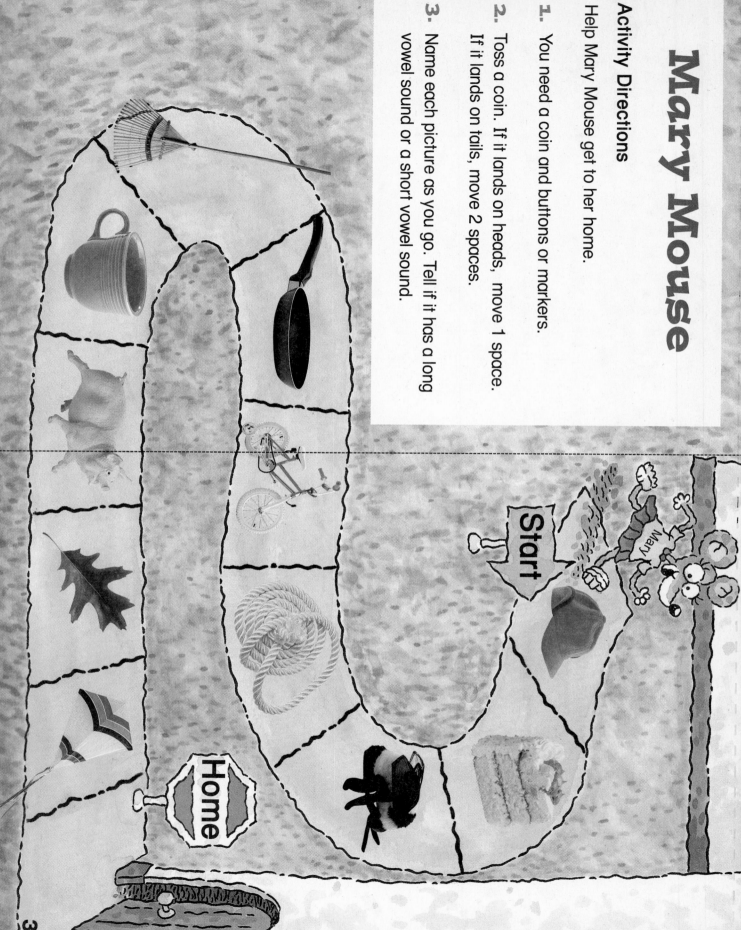

cap   cake

 Color.

 Directions: Name each picture. Color the pictures that have a long vowel sound, blue and those with a short vowel sound, red.

 Home Activity: Have your child name the pictures that have a long *i* sound.

© Scott Foresman K

Phonics: Long Vowels **277**

Name _____

 Circle.  Color.

 Write the letter that makes this an action word.

r _ _ _ ke

 Directions: Circle the mouse that *climbs* up the stool and the mouse that *rakes*. Color the mouse that *eats*.

 Home Activity: Ask your child to describe what each mouse is doing in the pictures that are not circled or colored.

© Scott Foresman K

278 Grammar: More Action Words (Verbs)

Draw.

Directions: Draw a picture showing how the mouse felt about the mess. Tell about your picture.

 Home Activity: Ask your child to tell you why this picture makes sense.

Comprehension: Drawing Conclusions **279**

 Circle.

a e i o u   a e i o u   a e i o u

a e i o u   a e i o u   a e i o u

Think Name a word that rhymes with **beet**.
What long vowel sound do you hear?

_____

- - - - - - - - - - -

_____

 Directions: Say the picture name. Circle the letter that stands for the long vowel sound you hear in the name.

 Home Activity: Help your child name words with the long *o* sound. *(rope, boat, soap, float,* and *note)*

© Scott Foresman K

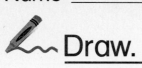 Draw.

 Directions: Pretend you are a mouse. Draw the food you would like to eat. Did you make a mess like Mouse did?

 Home Activity: Have your child tell you about the mess that Mouse made in *Mouse Mess*.

Name _____

  Circle.

   **Ee   Ii   Aa   Uu**

 Draw a line.

 Aa

like	bat	look	up
to	my	tug	yellow

 Directions: Circle the letters for the long vowel sound in *rake*. Name the pictures. Circle the picture that has the same long vowel sound as *cube*. Draw a line under the picture that has the long *a* sound. Draw a line under the words *look* and *to*.

282 Phonics: Assessment

© Scott Foresman K

Family Times

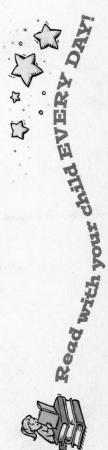

If You Add

If you add an **r** to a word like fog,
F-r-o-g now spells frog.

If you add an **l** to a word like cap,
C-l-a-p now spells clap.

If you add an **r** to a word like dip,
D-r-i-p now spells drip.

If you add an **r** to a word like tap,
T-r-a-p now spells trap.

Fog to frog, cap to clap,
Dip to drip, tap to trap!

This rhyme uses words that have consonant blends, such as *fr, dr,* and *cl.* Recite "If You Add" with your child.

(fold here)

Name: _____

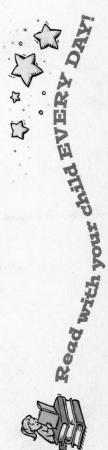

1

You are your child's first and best teacher!

Here are ways to help your child practice skills while having fun!

Day 1 Help your child find words in the rhyme on page 1 that begin with two letters, such as *cl* or *fr*.

Day 2 Together, look for words that begin with *fr; tr; dr; br; cl* or *pl* in one of your child's favorite books.

Day 3 Read a favorite story with your child. Ask your child to tell what happened in the beginning, the middle, and the end of the story.

Day 4 Your child is practicing acting out stories and poems. Encourage your child to playact a favorite story character.

Day 5 Your child is learning about words that name more than one. Have your child help name items that are more than one to add to a grocery list or serve for a special meal.

Read with your child EVERY DAY!

4

Phonics Game: On the Track

Game Directions

Play with a partner.

1. Make a spinner with a paper clip and a pencil.

2. Take turns. Spin the paper clip with your finger. Name a word that begins with the letters the spinner lands on.

3. Move a marker the number of spaces shown on the spinner.

4. The first one to reach the end of the track wins.

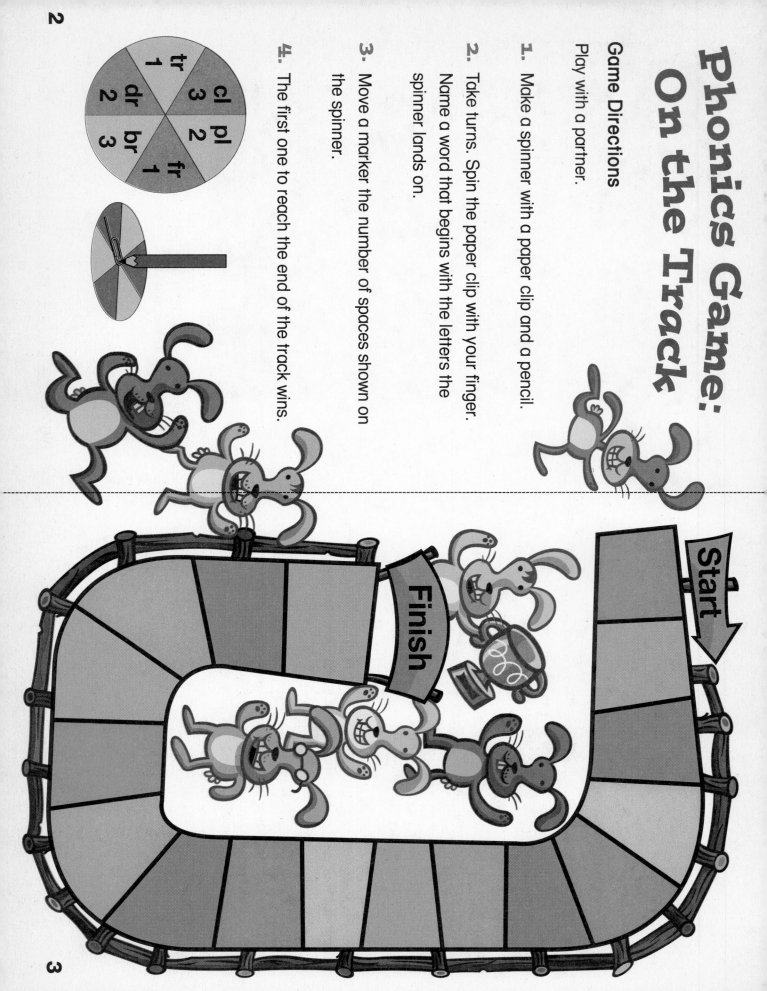

Start

Finish

Name _____

tr    fr

 Circle.

 Write the letters fr. _____

Write the letters tr. _____

 Directions: Name each picture. Circle the picture with blue if it begins with *tr* and with red if it begins with *fr*.

 Home Activity: Help your child name other words that begin with *fr* or *tr*.

Name _____

 Draw a line.

chicken

chickens

girl

girls

plate

plates

apple

apples

 Directions: Look at each picture. Draw a line under the naming word that matches the picture.

 Home Activity: Have your child use one of the underlined words in a sentence.

© Scott Foresman K

Circle.

 Draw.

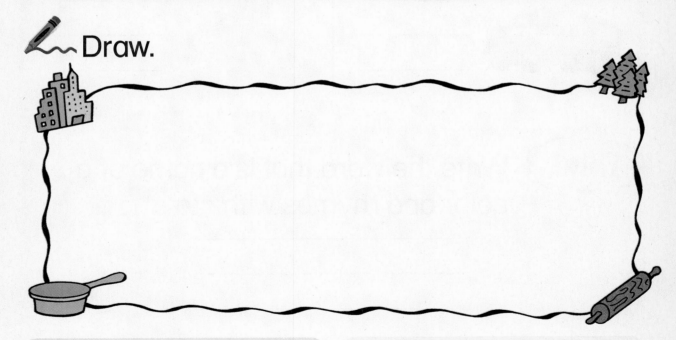

Directions: Circle the picture that shows where part of the story takes place. Draw a picture about the end of the story.

Home Activity: Ask your child to tell you what happened in the story *The Wolf's Chicken Stew*.

Comprehension: Story Elements **287**

Name _____

tr    **cl**

 _____    _____

 _____   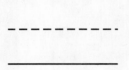 _____

 _____    _____

Think Write the word that is a name of a color and rhymes with **clown**.

_____

_____

 Directions: Say the name of each picture. Write the two beginning letters.

 **Home Activity:** Have your child name something in your home that begins with *br*.

Name _____

✏️ Draw.

_____

- -

_____

- -

_____

Directions: Draw how you would feel if you were a chick in *The Wolf's Chicken Stew*. Write a thank-you note to Uncle Wolf.

 Home Activity: Ask your child to tell about a favorite part of *The Wolf's Chicken Stew*.

Circle.

    cr   fr   tr   br

  |

 Draw a line.

pl

sp

pr

Directions: Circle the two letters that begin the word *frog*. Name the pictures. Circle the picture that begins with the same two letters as *cracker*. Draw a line under the picture that begins with the letters at the left.

Family Times

Funny Bunny

Funny Bunny's mom said,
"Mop, mop, mop."
Funny Bunny thought she said,
"Hop, hop, hop!"

Funny Bunny's mom said,
"Wash the pan."
Funny Bunny thought she said,
"Play with the van!"

Funny Bunny's mom said,
"Take a nap."
Funny Bunny thought she said,
"Clap and tap!"

Funny Bunny's mom said,
"Eat your fig."
Funny Bunny thought she said,
"Do a jig!"

This rhyme features rhyming words with the short vowels. Read "Funny Bunny" with your child. You may want to read the first two lines of each verse and ask your child to supply the second two lines.

(fold here)

Name: _____

You are your child's first and best teacher!

Here are ways to help your child practice skills while having fun!

Day 1 Help your child identify the rhyming words in "Funny Bunny."

Day 2 Make up rhyming riddles for your child to answer, and encourage your child to make up riddles for you. Your riddles can follow this pattern: "What word starts with *d* and rhymes with *pig*?"

Day 3 Read a story together. Afterward, talk with your child about the characters in the story. Ask questions about the characters' personalities.

Day 4 Give your child practice in communicating messages. Tell your child a message. Then have your child go to another room and retell the message to a different member of the family.

Day 5 Your child is learning to write sentences. Write simple notes to your child and encourage your child to write similar notes to you.

Read with your child EVERY DAY!

Phonics Game:
Rhyming Words

Game Directions

Play this game with a friend or family member.

1. Move box by box from the beginning to the end of the picture trail.

2. Take turns naming the picture and saying a word that rhymes with the picture word.

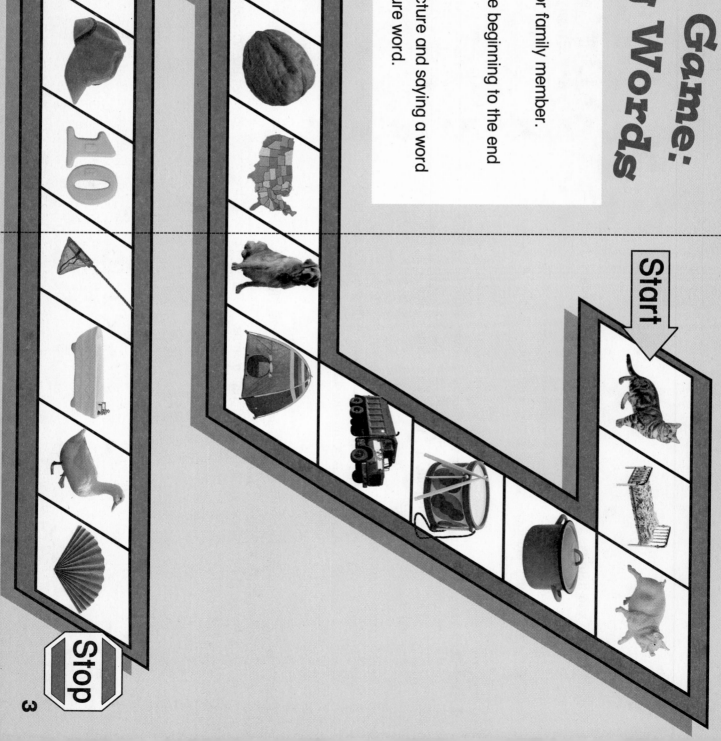

Start

Stop

10

Name _____

 Circle.

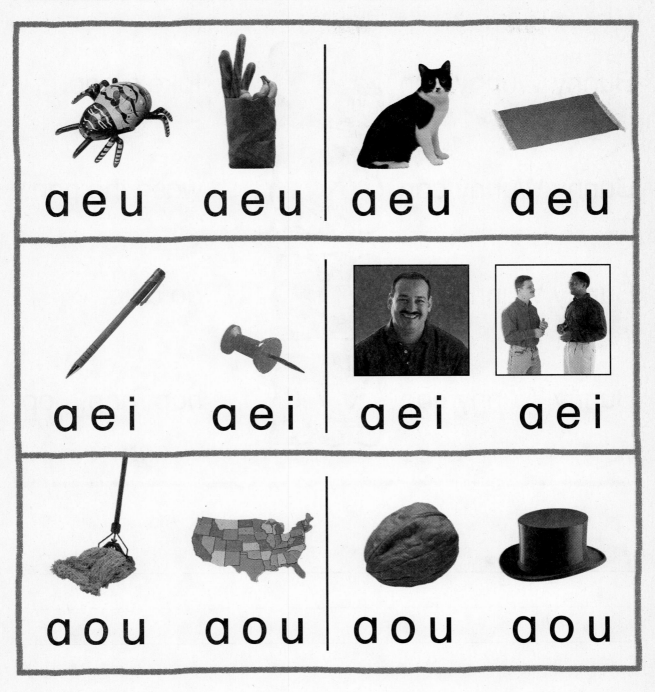

a e u   a e u   a e u   a e u

a e i   a e i   a e i   a e i

a o u   a o u   a o u   a o u

 Think Name a word that has a short *o* sound.

 Directions: Name the pictures in each box. Circle the letter that stands for the middle sound in each name.

Home Activity: Ask your child to name the short vowel sound in each word.

Draw a line.

Bunny Wunny can  take a nap.

Bunny Wunny can  wash the pan.

Bunny Wunny can  do a jig.

Bunny Wunny can  hop, hop, hop.

✏️ **Write.**

_____

- -

_____

- -

_____

 Directions: Look at each picture. Draw a line to finish each sentence. Then copy one sentence on the lines at the bottom.

Home Activity: Have your child read the completed sentences on this page.

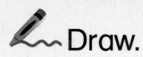 Draw.

Please bring
me a dish.

Please get your hat.

Directions: Read what Buddy's parents say. Draw a picture to show what Buddy might bring if he isn't listening.

 Home Activity: Ask your child to tell what happened to Buddy in *Listen Buddy*.

Comprehension: Drawing Conclusions **295**

© Scott Foresman K

Name _____

 Circle.

 Write a word that has a long **a** sound.

_____

- -

_____

 Directions: Say each picture name. Circle the pictures that have a long vowel sound.

 Home Activity: Have your child name the pictures that have short vowels.

© Scott Foresman K

296 Phonics: Skill Review

My Little Book

This little book belongs to

_____

Directions: Write your name.

✂ (cut here)

1

This is my p _____ .

3

(fold here)

the end

Now it is time to e _____ it!

8

This is my t _____ .

6

This is my p _ _ _ _ _ .

This is my _ _ _ o-yo.

Directions: Tell what you see. Write the missing letters.

This is my c _ _ _ pe.

This is my n _ _ _ _ _ .

 Directions: Draw a picture of what Buddy might bring if his parents asked for a pan.

 Home Activity: Talk with your child about things you will do this summer.

Circle.

 Draw a line.

i

o

Directions: Circle the pictures that have the same middle sound as in *fan*. Circle those that have the same vowel as in *hen*. Circle those that have the same long vowel as in *rose*. Draw a line under those that have the letter *i* in the middle; *o* in the middle.